# From This World, Another

DAVID ROTHENBERG

STEPHEN NACHMANOVITCH

Terra Nova Editions          2021

ISBN 978-1-949597-24-0

editor: Tyran Grillo
cover photo:  a nuthatch oracle at Delphi
set in Spectrum and Calibri

Terra Nova Editions
Second Printing


www.terranovapress.com

# From This World,
# Another

FROM THIS WORLD,

*Stephen Nachmanovitch and David Rothenberg share an affinity for improvising music, thinking about improvisation, and the songs of birds. Quarantined this past year like the rest of us, they decided to make an album together online.*

*How best to release it?*
*How to know what it is we may be hearing?*

*The two of us, writers as well as players, decided to talk our way through the music, and the ideas behind the music, and speak a book together.*

*This is the result.*

# What Can Be Said About Music?

DR: What can be said about music? What can be said about improvisation? I often have a lot of questions. On my favorite label, ECM, the improvised albums have *no* information about the music—maybe where it was recorded, who did it, but not any discussion. I've always preferred improvised music to composed music. And yet, sometimes I question my own preference. Am I just not serious enough?

SN: The difference between improvised music and composed music is pretty fuzzy. All music is a hybrid process: improvising-composing-improvising-composing. When we take recordings of our improvisations and fix them up in the computer, snip little bits off and fluff them up to give them a nice sound, that's already composition.

DR: Yes. The process of making and shaping this record involves, of course, a lot of composition.

SN: We improvised our music together over Zoom while simultaneously recording our own tracks on our own computers with good equipment. Using the Zoom video as a reference, we later synchronized our separate tracks, and presto, we have high-quality audio created remotely. One of the fascinating things about this process is that in editing the music we can use tools that are usually not available in improvised music but are available in tightly structured pop music and rock where, for example, the drummer records in a booth and the singer records in another booth. The sounds are isolated and then put together in editing. If there's a blooper in one person's line, you can fix it without changing the other person's line. You can get a more refined recording than you often can in the context of live improvisation where we're playing together in the same room.

DR: In improvisation, and a lot of music that doesn't emphasize being improvised, you learn from the musicians who were there together, making something. A lot of pop music is made that way—people just get together and play and they're bringing something and nobody tells them exactly what to do. I think those who are promoting improvisation have to remind people that, in fact, most of the world's music is made like that.

SN: Notated music is just a sliver on top of thousands of years of improvised music.

DR: Absolutely. We compose with sound the way John Cage and Glenn Gould said people were going to be doing this in the future. They're going to take the sound and work with it. We are now in that future! They both thought that would be a sign of elite contemporary music. They didn't quite get that it would be popular music that would run wild with this. Still, in the world of classical music, people tend to trust the score. The very fact that something is written down, it gives it ...

SN: ... this religious, serious flavor. My friend, the conductor Larry Livingston, said that the difference between improvisation and composition is between *no*tation and *yes*tation.

DR: Is the line really so fuzzy? We have these great musicians who play written music and other people who don't read music and play great music, but they don't start from the written notes at all. There is a difference in paradigm.

## GUIDO AND TOM

SN: I like to talk about Guido and Tom. To me, the two most important dates in the history of Western music are 1025 and 1876. In 1025, Guido of Arezzo invented music notation, which is the digital representation of sound.

DR: What did he notate? What was the first notated music?

SN: It was church music.

DR: Is there a single first example? Did he wake up and say, today I'm writing this down?

SN: People invented notational systems before, the neumes of the Middle Ages that gave a rough graphical sense of how music went, but Guido invented the modern system of the five-line staff, with notes and stems representing exact pitches and exact durations. The interesting thing about notation is that it's digital: that is, you can have an A or a B flat, but in between you're nowhere. The crack between them is no-man's land.

I've got a couple of pictures up on the wall. On the left, medieval Tibetan music notation. On the right, the first page of Yehudi Menuhin's score to Bach's Sonata No. 2 in A minor.

Menuhin's Bach: scribbles over scribbles. Here is the sacred notation of Bach, which must not be tampered with, but it's covered with scribbles! The printed score on which he scribbled is digital because each note is either a sixteenth note or an eighth note or a dotted eighth or whatever; it's either an A natural or a B flat. But, of course, if you look at Bach's original manuscript of the Sonatas and Partitas, they were incredibly flowing, squishy, calligraphic representations of this notation. Compare this to Tibetan musical notation. That's a lot squishier and was never digital.

DR: How interesting that you have precisely those two images up on the wall. I used the exact same two images in an essay I wrote for an exhibition entitled *Drawing Sound*. I went to Nepal to study that stuff.

SN: So, in 1025, we have the digital representation of music in the form of notation. The advantage of digital representation of anything, regardless of the medium, is that it's portable and relatively small. You can write music notation on a piece of paper, fold it up, put it in your pocket, and give it to somebody to teach to his or her students in another town. And that's how music spread in the centuries after the Middle Ages.

The disadvantage of notation is that it's all-or-nothing. It perpetuated the idea of the right notes versus the wrong notes, or the classics that are written down versus the impure things that are made up on the fly.

Then, in 1876, Thomas Edison invented the analog representation of music. On the phonograph record, the needle incises a wave on the medium—originally a wax cylinder or later disc—that's an analog representation of the sound. The wiggles on the disc are *analogs* of the wiggles of the sound waves.

DR: Can you actually get the sound the same way photography captures a moment in an image as a painting never could do?

SN: Right. You hear the sound from a particular moment in time. Even if the recording is degraded like a scratched LP, it is an analog, a picture, of sound. Now we use computers and other recorders that digitize the waveforms, but recording is still a representation of the sound waves. The symbols of notation are still more compact, as MIDI is, but you lose the actual sound and have to try to reconstruct it in performance. We're able to communicate through computers because the analog of our voices and our faces is digitized temporarily in, as that elderly senator from Alaska called it, "the intertubes that connect us."

So, here's the question: What if we lived on a planet where those two dates of Guido and Tom were reversed, 1025 and 1876—a planet where recording came *before* notation? How might culture have developed differently if people in past centuries could have recorded music and heard music without digitizing it into notation and having to decode the difference between an A and a B flat.

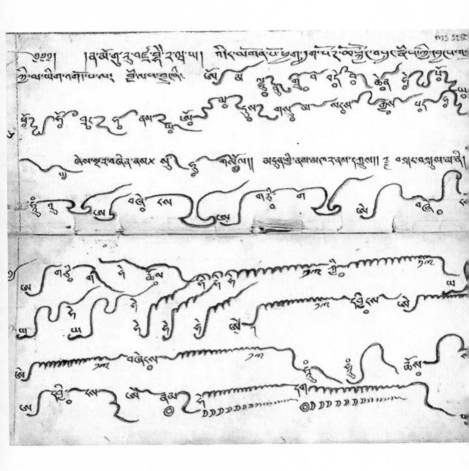

DR: Don't you think it kind of *is* that way for a lot of people in a lot of music cultures around the world? These are places where music has never been written down but is still passed down from generation to generation. When they first got recordings, they could hear what they sounded like and say, "Oh, okay, that's interesting." And they would learn it all orally with recordings they could use. And then, someone later said, "If you write it down, it becomes more serious." When I went to Nepal, armed with that Tibetan notation you have on your wall, I said, "How come you don't have any notation for the wind instrument music?" My teacher, Lama Sangye Tenzin, said, "Why would we bother? We just teach it to you." I told the lama, "In the West, if it's written down, it's taken more seriously."

He agreed to invent some written notation for me. I wrote about this in my book *Sudden Music* and in this unpublished Tibetan music article where I talk about my whole rather unrigorous process. He invented this notation for melodies because the neumatic notation is for the inflection of chanted sacred words. They didn't need notation to pass this tradition over the generations. They were already using tape recorders to teach the baby monks the old ways. They would record the *gyaling*, the wind instrument I studied, on a tape recorder, take it home, and practice without notation. Notation came later among those who wanted to analyze the traditions.

SN: The same thing happened with dance notation. In the twentieth century, choreographers wanted to be recognized as real artists, and therefore said, "We must have notation." So, now, there are several systems of choreographic notation that have been developed. And they're all, of course, very sketchy in both senses of the word, because you can't really notate dance, though it's helpful to draw rough diagrams. Notation is something you must learn in order to be recognized in academia and be recognized as a high art form. But, of course, dance has always been a high art form that shouldn't need anybody's approval or standardization.

There are so many byways we can follow here. What do they call it in North African cities, the Medina?

DR: Like the Grand Bazaar of Istanbul. The original shopping mall ... of ideas.


## ... AND JOHN


SN: This is how the mind can work. John Cage told me he did not like improvisation. I talk about that a little bit in my book *The Art of Is.* However, he gave birth to so many ideas that have liberated improvisational musicians, that have helped creative musicians on the edge between notation and improvisation to wiggle a little more freely on that borderline.

At one point he's talking about an episode where Leonard Bernstein invited him to do something with the New York Philharmonic. The orchestra was grumbling. John said that they got riled up at "what they were obliged to do." Here's a composer whose ideology is full of human freedom, but he's still telling the players, *you are obliged to be free* in the way I prescribe.

DR: Cage still believed in being a composer. And this was the era of composers having this tremendous power like Boulez and Stockhausen and Cage, who at least was this figure of lightness, who made people open up, even though they might start to laugh when he was telling them what he wanted them to do—turn on radios and make funny sounds and the like ...

SN: Exactly.

DR: I'm sure you've seen the film where John Cage is juxtaposed with Rahsaan Roland Kirk, both wandering around London. It's called *Sound??* and it was made in 1967 by Dick Fontaine. In the film, they never meet each other. They were there, filmed around the same time. In a lot of it, John Cage seems like a mad jazz musician, and Rahsaan seems like this erudite philosopher of music. And yet Cage came out of this world where a composer is supposed to be someone serious, who wanted to distinguish themselves from these unserious people like jazz musicians who were considered popular artists. The notion that that world could produce serious art was somewhat threatening to him. Yet jazz has mostly been an unpopular kind of popular music. Jazz musicians are people looking for new ideas; many loved Cage's ideas. John Cage convinced me as a teenager that I could do anything I wanted—no wonder I couldn't be a classical musician. He was wonderfully inspiring. And I don't think he was angry when people didn't do things his way. He was much more of an improviser than he would admit to being...

SN: I remember this one conversation with him, where he was

telling me about how much he disliked the idea of improvisation. He felt that improvisation expressed your personal knowledge, feelings, and predilections and he wanted his music to get beyond those personal elements. That's why he liked to compose with randomizing elements like the *I Ching* or tossing coins. So I brought up the subject of mushrooms with him. As you know, he was an avid collector of mushrooms and an accomplished mycologist. Do you know how he became a collector of mushrooms?

DR: I know he won a lot of money on a quiz show in Italy answering questions about them.

SN: When he was an undergraduate at Pomona College, he had a professor who said, "John, you're too single-mindedly focused on music. You should broaden your interests." So, already being John Cage, he went home and picked up a pocket dictionary and looked up the word *music* and looked right above it in the dictionary. He saw the word *mushroom* and said, "Okay, I'll learn about those."

So I asked him, "John, when you go out into the country and collect mushrooms and you decide which ones to eat and which ones are poisonous, do you toss coins or throw the *I Ching*, or do you use your knowledge and feeling for mushrooms?" And he just sat back and gave me this big grin.

DR: Cage thought improvisation was like a conversation. He didn't think music should be a conversation.

SN: Well, personally, I kind of like conversations. And so today, here we are!

DR: I sense that he wanted to be a composer among composers, people with the power to tell us what music is. If your music is made by a method that he perceived as not being planned out, he felt, I believe, that would be cheapening it, turning it into some sort of free-for-all. That is one way people misunderstand improvisation. And I would say that much of my music is constantly misunderstood by people. They're still waiting for the *song*. They're waiting for the melody, the structure. When I make all these films and concerts with birds, some people ask, "What are you doing here? Where's the song? I want you to play a song with the bird." That would make it like music for them. And I keep saying, "No, no, no, that's boring."

In many nature films with humpback whale songs, the whale song is played for about ten seconds at most before the guitars, the synthesizers, and the Hans Zimmer-scored orchestra come in. But I would prefer that we just deal with reality here. This is music. As in *The Treasure of the Sierra Madre*, "This is the real world, muchachos, and we are in it!" Listen to it, take the viewer seriously; you're going to hear all kinds of cool stuff. You don't have to turn it into the immediate familiar.

SN: Exactly.

## TAKE ADVANTAGE OF WHAT *IS*

DR: I think you have to believe that improvisation leads to results. I was very impressed by the *New Yorker* profile of Jason

Moran from a few years ago where they're introducing this great jazz musician, artist, organizer. But then Alec Wilkinson writes, the main thing about Jason Moran is he believes that "improvisation lets you create music that can be created no other way." Like you have to use this method to get this music—very simply, it's a technique that gets results. And I think all people who believe in improvisation pretty much believe that.

SN: Well, it *is* a technique that gets results. And one of the great things is that, if you create, if you improvise for five minutes, you will have created a five-minute piece of music that took five minutes to create. If you want to notate a five-minute piece of music, it might take weeks.

DR: So that's why the composer thinks they're better. They've put in all those hours ...

SN: To me, the composer is neither better nor worse than the improviser—they are two parallel ways to get to music. In all the pieces that we created for this album, we did little bits of editing and snipping on them. That brought us into the compositional realm. But it's still a very efficient way of producing stuff because the basic ideas and the dialogue and the conversation between us took place in real time. The funny thing is that it then takes much longer to think of names for the pieces than it does to create them!

DR: Titles in music always take a little bit away from musical experience. The composer who writes music down might write something that ends up sounding just like what we made, but something about the process of composition believes that that's worth doing. I've written only one completely written-down solo piece for clarinet. It's called "Pibroch" and is based on Scottish formal bagpipe music. It was performed for the first time a month or two ago in New York City in a kind of streamed lockdown concert by these two clarinetists. It was years ago that I wrote it—1987!—and it was such a different process and also very hard to get them to play it the way I imagined it simply because not enough precise instructions were written down. But my tendency was to tell them, "Do what you want with it, play it slow, play it fast. I don't care, make it your own." And then they said, "Can you just play it for us, record it yourself?" I took a look at the score, all the intricate multiphonic fingerings, and I said, "No, I don't want to play that. It's for you, not me." I wrote that down years ago. It's for those who want to read music, not those who want to improvise.

SN: My eye was once caught by a marking on the score of Carl Nielsen's Fifth Symphony. Classical composers usually write a tempo marking at the head of each movement—they'll say *Allegro* for fast or *Lento* for very slow or whatever. But at the head of this symphony, Nielsen wrote *Tempo giusto*: the right tempo.

DR: That's fine.

SN: He's saying, "Okay folks, it's in your court now."

DR: I sometimes think these composers have a point: there must *be* something more serious in this worked-out composed music, something I don't quite get, or I don't have the patience enough for, to grasp these large structures. These symphonies might go on for up to an hour. These carefully written things ...

I like to know if the music is made up as it's being played. I follow improvisation more closely, even though I started out being interested in written music and grew up in a family where if it was classical music, it was serious. These other things are fine, but they're less serious than classical music. My parents said, "You should be a composer or a conductor." Leonard Bernstein's parents also worried about him. They said, "What to do? My son wants to be a *klezmer*! There's no future in that."

I gravitated to this kind of jazz that was free but also kind of melodic and spirited, this ECM European sound, which I thought of also as a kind of elite thing ...

SN: I gravitate toward exactly the same thing, which is why we've been having fun playing together.

DR: Yes. And my friends didn't. I thought I was special, that I was on to something other people didn't get. I was kind of arrogant and I had a lot of people mad at me. I didn't quite say, "This is better than what you like," but I kind of felt that there was some special thing here. I guess, like John Cage, I was an elitist in my own way ...

SN: As a consumer of music or as a fan of music, I adore Western classical music and I love those big composed architectural structures. I love listening to them now just as much as I loved listening to them sixty years ago. But it's just not what

I feel like doing myself. I certainly appreciate it, just as I like straight-ahead jazz or bebop. I love listening to it, but it's not what I want to *do*. The world is so is full of such a huge menu of things that we can appreciate. You don't have to say one thing is better or worse. It's just a matter of: What's in your hands? What's in your elbows? What do you want to make?

DR: This suddenly reminds me of the summer of 1980, when I was studying at the Naropa Institute with the band Oregon— Glen Moore, Paul McCandless, Ralph Towner, and Collin Walcott. There was a student, this guy named Sam Gulisano. He's still around, in the Bay Area. And he made the largest piece, the most epic work of the summer, just one melody. He played a berimbau, the Brazilian instrument, and he sang on top of the sound *by, by, bidi bidi, by, by, bidi, by, by*, just one rhythm repeating on and on. Everyone joined in with this kind of Terry Riley *In C* quality. There was no deep composition, but it was a huge evolving piece that went on for an hour. And when it was done, we all felt like we were part of something special, something I would never forget. I can't remember how he composed or improvised it, but I think mostly he was just sort of signaling: you play this, then you play that. And it totally worked as a large form. It's the one piece of music I remember best from that summer long ago, even though there were a lot of people, myself included, writing complicated tunes with strange dissonant chords. But this one thing I remember, because it was this enveloping spiritual experience. Forty years later, these borders between improvisation, between the classical and the psychedelic, have seriously faded.

SN: They've faded. And that's a good thing. If we don't destroy civilization and if we don't destroy the ecosystem (I'll give us a 50-50 on that), we're living in a kind of renaissance or golden age of culture right now. Although there are many bad things about the internet, one of the great things about it is that you can get up in the morning and read a description of what someone is doing in Turkmenistan or wherever and instantly find it and hear it.

DR: You and I both remember how hard it was to find these secret musics, like when George Crumb told me how he wrote *Vox Balaenae*: "Oh, there was this one tape of whale songs that went around, passed around from musician to musician." If you can imagine the era, only some people would have the tape and have to lend it to others—whereas now, anything you want to hear, you can hear. And then, at the same time, people still complain music's all too much the *same* everywhere. Why do they still say that? They don't know how to delve into these mysterious things. And there are so many mysterious things.

SN: What we have to do is encourage people to take advantage of what *is*.

DR: And this is why curation is on the rise. Curators are considered so important today because they know how to direct people through the morass, at least in theory. It's easier than ever before to record something wonderful. Release it to the world, get people to listen to it—but to make it seem to *matter* is so much harder.

SN: That is hard. It's partly due to the fact that in the days of the classical composers, the classical poets, or whatever art form you want to consider, the world's population was much smaller and the portion of the population that read books was much smaller. The portion of the population that *might* have written books but had no access to cultural resources due to class, gender, place of birth—that's another issue. But, in any case, you could say that in early nineteenth-century England there were half a dozen major poets and you can name them. Thus, we have the dead white men, one strand of literature. But now the population of the world is enormous and the resources that are available to many people to create art are enormous. It's no longer only the white men; it's all kinds of people from whom we finally get to hear. And so the range of styles, the range of formats, and the range of languages is gigantic. This is all great!

It means there isn't going to be a canon anymore; no longer will we be able to say here are the six or seven people who are revered. The big press, *The New York Times* or whatever, is still going to want to mention the dozen most important composers in America. But, in reality, that's been completely exploded. There are myriad significant composers in America and no one person will know them all.

DR: Yes, the press will end up missing out, of course. There will always be something else that's interesting that never gets mentioned.

## WHAT'S THIS MUSIC FOR?

DR: We often wonder: What is all this cultural production *for*? What's all this music for? I have noticed that in a world where everything streams endlessly, people tend to look to their music for a function: This song will help me relax. This one will help me study. This one will help me dance. Spotify itself pushes this philosophy, saying, "We're going to end all genre. Music is now what the people want whenever they want. It doesn't matter whether it's jazz or rock or hip hop—it's just music to enhance your life."

Is music making me happier when it wakes me up when I need to wake up? Everything becomes functional. My students think of music that way. They hear something and they go, "What am I supposed to do with this? What's it for?" In some classes, I've given students this entire book by Greil Marcus on one Bob Dylan song, *Like a Rolling Stone*. First, they can't imagine how anyone could write an entire book on a single song. Second, they can't imagine that a song could matter as much as he tries to describe it mattering. They just think music isn't that kind of thing anymore. It couldn't be. And I wonder if that's true, and is it a good or bad or happy or sad thing if music doesn't matter the way it once did?

SN: Purpose, purpose. I'm writing something now about purpose, *against* purpose. Against the so-called purpose-driven life. I have a piece of writing called "Galumphing Fifty Years On."

DR: What was the original galumphing?

SN: The original galumphing was a paper that I wrote fifty years ago when I was …

DR: … at the Institute of Galumphing Studies …

SN: … in William James Hall at Harvard University, studying the play of baby baboons and baby children, and discovering the pattern that I called *galumphing*, which is this: in play, you don't go from here to there; you jump and you dance from here to there and you do all this exuberant, unnecessary movement. To do things that are unnecessary and that don't have a purpose *is the essence of life*. And here we are, you and I, doing it. We have the preacher who writes about the purpose-driven life, saying that you've got to have a purpose. And if you don't know what it is, I can tell you what God's purpose for you is— in return for the following fee.

DR: My philosophy professor Erazim Kohák used to say, "In God we trust. All others pay cash." And he was a philosopher of religion!

SN: When budgets for music in the schools are cut and people try to restore the money, they try to justify it in terms of "music is good for cognitive development." There was that horrible "Mozart Effect," remember, back in the nineties? This always made me want to believe in zombies, that the zombie of Mozart would rise from his pauper's grave outside of Vienna and come to the United States and eat the brains of the people who invented the Mozart Effect. Here is the setup: you are a little kid, your parents have to justify your having a music course in school by saying that music makes you smart, meaning music will help you get better grades in schools. You'll get into a better high school so that you'll get into a better college so that you'll get a better job and make more money in your lifetime.

It all works out for the purpose of material gain. That's why music is supposedly valuable. The whole notion of value is such an unfortunate feature of our society, baked into almost everything that's done. For people to realize that you play to live and you live to play is a revolutionary act. We were talking the other day about bowerbirds and the birds of paradise—all the incredible multidisciplinary art forms that these birds do, this combination of music and dance and sculpture and architecture and theater, which I'm sure they don't think of in those compartments. In our framing of the birds' actions, it's all supposed to be for Darwinian sexual selection, meaning a serious purpose. The opposite view, which I prefer, is that Darwin and sexual selection and evolution serve creatures playing—to play, to be creative, to just spontaneously do what they want to do, and do it with others, and make the world more beautiful, *just because.*

DR: Everything in life is not driven toward function. Last year, two books came out about how one should do nothing. Doing nothing is good for you. They were reviewed together in *The New York Times* back in 2019.

SN: Yes, Jenny Odell, from Stanford: *How to Do Nothing.* That's a good book.

DR: Back then, I was going to some party in New York and I was in the elevator and started talking to this woman. I said, "Are you going to this party? Who are you?" She says, "I wrote a book on doing nothing." I said, "Did you write the book that said it was just good to do nothing or the book that said it's good to do nothing to help you become more productive in

life." She goes, "Mine was the one about just doing nothing."
"Good," I said.

That one is more honest because, of course, people think, just like studying music, daydreaming, doing nothing, makes you more productive, therefore it's good. But it is the notion of productivity itself that should be suspect.

SN: Yes!

DR: When you and I are making music, we record all this stuff and when we're done I put the computer down and go back in the house and say, "I have to do nothing now. We just made too much music." With the minimum of effort, we made stuff that sounds so beautiful and now it's time to do less. And so, sometimes, that does work on me.

SN: That was a great process because we ended up keeping eleven pieces and discarding three. Back to the *efficiency* of improvisation, you can make five minutes' worth of music in five minutes and it's there.

DR: See, it makes us more productive!

Of course, some people would cut and paste a lot more than we did. I think you and I both agreed that we didn't want to do too much of that. Unlike another record I did that came out recently called *Are We There Yet?* The band's called Cool Spring. Two days of recordings that I made in this house in 2018, or maybe even 2017. It was sitting around for years. No one was quite sure what to do with all these tracks and different people took hold of the session and started cutting and pasting. Finally, someone in Berlin took ahold of the whole thing and transformed it so that when it was done, I had barely a memory that this is what we played, what we did. Over time it was composed into something completely new, constructed—a Miles Davis / Teo Macero construction sort of thing.

People don't think of that as composition. *Bitches Brew* was the most popular Miles Davis album. It was basically all free improvisation. And it was cut and pasted into this kind of ambient jazz-rock fusion background that became an anthem of the era. People don't understand that that's *musique concrète*; that's composition, not only improvisation. Whether you like it or dislike it, it's certainly a composition made up out of the fragments of what jazz and rock are supposed to be. Music is sometimes this vague thing. The creative process is a mystery. This is something that used to bother me. If it was too easy to make something, it must not be serious. Then enough people told me, "That's so stupid." If one doesn't know how you make things, you can't even tell what value they have. You just have to do them whatever way it is you do. And you find that way.

SN: I'm thinking of the movie *Shakespeare in Love*—the Geoffrey Rush character has several episodes during the movie where things are completely falling apart. The first-ever performance of *Romeo and Juliet* will be a disaster. He keeps saying, "It will turn out well." The other person says "How?" and he says, "I don't know—it's a mystery." And it does turn out well.

Trusting the process, that's part of this enterprise, realizing that we're in something together. We all have our interests and we all have our flaws and we all have the things that we do better and worse, in a different coloration from each other. And yet, when we come together, as people of goodwill, it's a mystery, it just happens—something that has an interesting structure, that's different from what you do and different from what I do. It isn't a compromise or a meeting halfway between. It is something that happens from the alchemy of partners meeting.

## YOU MAKE ME LOOK GOOD

DR: One of the best things about improvisation is that it's often better done together with others. Strangely enough, during this lockdown world we're in, I have spent more time than ever collaborating with people far away. And then, even though many people I know say it's great to hunker down and do your own thing, it's when left alone that I get kind of antsy and tired of my own ideas. Then I'm stuck in circles. But when other people are brought in, that's when a kind of magic happens. I wonder if composers feel otherwise, that they feel like they have their ideas already, that they're for others to realize and follow?

SN: When we're improvising together, there's a degree to which we're copying each other, but, of course, we can't copy each other because we have different instruments and we're different personalities. The attempt to listen to and mirror each other in various ways results in this wonderful thing that isn't what I do and isn't what you do and isn't a compromise between us but is this whole new thing that arises from that mutual "copying."

DR: Increasingly I get more interested (unlike when I was younger) in this idea of doing things I don't entirely understand, together with other people like you, sharing the connection. It's only in the last of my music-nature projects, *Nightingales in Berlin*, that I emphasize *other* people. The best thing is to get someone else to go make music with a nightingale for the first time and listen to it, experience it, and join in.

SN: I really liked that aspect of the book a lot.

DR: Before I was just doing this weird stuff, out there alone against the elements. It was tiresome and not that interesting. And now, this is one thing that does excite me the most: bringing in more people who can do it. Now that I'm writing about underwater pond sounds, every time I hear someone in the world is making music out of underwater pond sounds, I contact them and call them up to find out how they relate to it. What are you doing? What are you thinking? And I'm putting all of that in this project.

SN: A lot of this may be personality types in terms of introverts versus extroverts. To sit alone and conceive and write and edit by yourself in a room, with the idea that this will be brought out to other people later, is still a way of interacting with other people, but in a different timeframe. Perhaps the most important statement about improvisation that I ever heard was from the acting teacher Del Close, who said that in theater, "Your job as an improviser is not to come up with clever lines. Your job as an improviser is to make your part-ner's shitty lines sound good." Keith Johnstone called this *chivalry*. For people who are creative and educated and know a lot of stuff, it's very easy for us to get stuck in the stuff that we know or become excessively proud of what we know. That's when I try to remember that when you're playing with somebody else, your job is to make *them* look good.

DR: Do you think that works for music as well?

SN: It absolutely does. Even in the most traditional string quartets or orchestras, they say if you can't hear your neighbor playing, you're playing too loud.

DR: That's right. People tend to mix themselves too loud in the studio because they're so obsessed with themselves! So, if you mix yourself, when done, always turn yourself down. It's always too damn high!

SN: What you think you need to do is often not what you need.

DR: Sidney Bechet would practice scales, arpeggios, and mel-odies on his balcony in Paris. At some point, he would stop doing that and just make weird animal noises. Once a neigh-bor said, "Sidney, what's going on? What are you playing there?" He sighed, "Sometimes what we call music is not the *real* music." This was a musician who was a traditionalist! I read that in a David Toop book, I think ...

SN: There is an everyday definition of improvisation—dealing with emergencies—which is, of course, what we're going to have more and more of as the twenty-first century goes on. We didn't choose to be living in a world that's having these problems. You didn't choose to run your car off the road and get stuck in the snow, but you're here, so how will you respond to it? You're here with other people who may be very different from you.

DR: People tend to think improvising means dealing with challenges when you *don't have a plan*, but those who believe in it think it means being able to deal with something you don't expect by being ready for things to go differently than you expected. It's like expecting to teach a class for fifty people and it turns out only one person shows up: okay, we must adjust to this. Or a musician was supposed to show up with a violin but they show up with a tuba and you work with it. You're ready for the unexpected, rather than just flailing.

People who don't like improvisation say it sounds like they're just flailing about not paying attention to anything.

SN: Well, sometimes they are. There is good improvisation and bad improvisation, just as there's good composed music and bad composed music. People will differ as to how they define or perceive those. To me, good improvisation depends on listening. I have seen and played with people who are just playing their instrument and that's it; it doesn't matter who they're with and it doesn't matter what the other people are doing. "I'm gonna do it, I'm gonna let my feelings out."

DR: Some people have that as their ethos. They say, "It's not really improvisation unless you're detached from all genre, all tradition."

SN: Being chivalrous toward the people you're around doesn't mean you don't challenge them. Nor does it mean you don't constantly try out new things, but you also say something and give it time to land. And then, when it's landed, you can say something else and give that time to land and have some sense that you're engaged in reciprocity with everyone around you, rather than, "I'm great and I'm just going to listen to myself expand."

DR: I feel like the best free improvisers lure you in, like my teacher Joe Maneri. He would always win over the audience. He was this crazy clarinetist and atonal composer, but sometimes I would bring friends to hear his improvised concerts, and he would win them over just by being so warm, sometimes just singing in a made-up language. He lured in the people, whereas other people would make you feel like they're just doing their thing with no regard for the audience.

One class of nightingales sings as if no one else is around. Like they just don't care who is listening. They're oblivious. "Wasn't that divine? Don't I sound wonderful?" Whereas most others are listening for responses, leaving space for the other birds to join in, acknowledging that everyone has their own territory and their place.

Some people evolve. You hear them once and then again and notice decades later they've mellowed out and gotten much humbler and become a whole different kind of musician.

## FELDMAN AND SLOWING DOWN

SN: I'm seventy years old. I remember when I was half my current age, still living in L.A. There was an event at Cal Arts that featured Morton Feldman. At that time, I didn't know anything about him or his music. He spoke and played. I thought it was the most boring thing I'd ever heard in my life, just these incredibly sparse chords with a huge amount of space between them. I was already a meditator, but somehow I didn't make the connection. Now I *adore* Feldman's music and I'm impatient with things like Paganini or bebop virtuosos. These are people who can play very fast and impress you with their technique. It's technically impressive but not very interesting, whereas things that are slower and have breath can touch me now.

I have a friend named Ken Fischer who ran the College Music Society at the University of Michigan for many years. He was taking me on a tour of the campus. They have this huge bell tower, one of the biggest carillons in the world. He let me sit up there and play the carillon for a little while. I'd never done anything like that before. Sometimes you walk by a campus or some other facility that has a carillon and somebody's playing a tune with a lot of notes, as though they were playing the piano. When I let the hammer go on this twelve-foot bell, its reverb time was enormous! Why would I play another note until it was finished? It was so interesting to let the sound slowly die out and mingle with the space around me. Why step on it by making lots of gestures just to prove that you can make lots of gestures? I think that does have something to do with age because it's natural for a young organism to be galumphing more, jittering and frittering around more, showing off what they can do.

DR: So what were you into back when you were disappointed by Morton Feldman?

SN: I was very interested in Keith Jarrett. I was very interested in Indian music and was studying it quite a bit. I was studying with Ali Akbar Khan. That is also a tradition that can get very, very slow and very deep. I was interested in jazz. I was interested in lots of things but somehow Morton didn't catch me. Then he caught me by remote control, thirty-five years later.

DR: I was always amazed at how few people play the way Keith Jarrett did in those days. He had his way of being simple and driving and kind of epic at the same time. So few pianists could pull that off. When others tried, they quickly got kind of new-agey, but Keith had something different.

SN: Only one person can play like that and only one person can play like you and only one person can play like me.

DR: But still, it was like a genre that, presumably, more people could have pursued if they wanted to.

SN: And people did want to, but they gave up. Keith also had a rare mixture of incredible technical chops and knowledge married with the kind of expressive freedom that no one else could match.

DR: Right. Of course, he remains a divisive figure. Lots of people think he is either too classical or fake gospelish. This may be why, later in life, he began to play more standards, to show that he truly is a jazz musician with amazing chops. But I like that trio most when they don't play standards. In a way, Chick Corea's standards are better, or at least more surprising. In the early days, Chick's band Circle was wilder than anything Jarrett ever did. But Jarrett has more gravitas. And he never became a Scientologist, of course …

SN: Chick was incredible. Since he died just last week, people have been sending clips back and forth of all the amazing things that he did throughout his life.

DR: So, you were into Keith Jarrett and Indian music. I could imagine myself at that stage having the same reaction to Morton Feldman. Like, what's the big deal? Why is he this heroic figure? But John Cage had the playfulness that you and I both liked. I have one friend, Mark Steven Brooks, who's obsessed with Feldman. He was in those classes Feldman taught in Buffalo. He has spent a lifetime in recovery from his study with Feldman, even remixing Feldman's speeches and music, cutting and pasting them into strange new forms.

My friend Damon Krukowski published a book of Feldman's writings on his imprint, Exact Change Press, back in the nineties. Krukowski wrote a more recent book himself called *The New Analog*, followed by a podcast based on it called *Ways of Hearing*. He's an alternative rock musician who made these interesting documents along the line of what you and I are doing. He investigates why we care about vinyl, why we care about print, and why the digital is never enough on its own.

## BATESON'S SENSE

DR: What do you think of John Cage saying that composing, performing, listening to music have nothing to do with one another? What do you think he meant by that?

SN: [Laughs] To me, composing, performing, and listening are intimately related and unified. That's the practice of music as I experience it.

DR: Why did he say it then?

SN: Cage's statement reminds me of Dōgen, the great thirteenth-century Japanese Zen philosopher. Dōgen said that fire has its own past, present, and future; wood has its own past, present, and future; and ashes have their own past, present, and future. Our experience of fire and wood, ashes and smoke, is that they're all phases of the same process and the same materials going through a transformation. When I was laughing at what Cage said, I realize that my own experience of music is that fire, wood, and smoke are all integral to this ongoing process. But they don't have to be. A person could write notation forever and not have it performed. A person can perform and never deal with notation. A person can listen and enjoy without knowing how the music is made. All of these activities can be separated, at least provisionally. But I like the idea of "musicking" from Christopher Small, by which he means to say that the listener, composer, performer, and, for that matter, the stagehands and others involved in the musical process are all musicking together. He was riffing off the ideas of my teacher, Gregory Bateson, who talked about stamping out nouns.

DR: He did?

SN: Everything is in motion. Everything that seems to be a solid separate entity is actually a verb. I'm a verb, you're a verb, music is a verb. My cells are constantly changing and this mind is being changed by the conversation that you and I are having now. Christopher Small talked about musicking as the unitary activity of listening, playing, composing, attending to, dancing to, bobbing your head to, even ignoring it—all of these activities are in some ways contiguous with each other, even though each person, in the moment, is only doing a snippet at a time.

Gregory's daughter Nora has a book called *Small Arcs of Larger Circles*. The title is riffing on her father's idea that what *looks* to us like a linear chain of cause-and-effect is in fact just a little arc of a larger circuit. This is the fundamental idea of ecology. The circle is entirely interconnected and you can't realistically separate the parts. But our habits of language predispose us to snip the circle into parts. We are part of an enormous system that includes all of humanity and all of creativity and all of nature. Gregory said that "life depends upon interlocking *circuits* of contingency, while consciousness can see only such short arcs of such circuits as human purpose may direct....What the unaided consciousness (unaided by art, dreams, and the like) can never appreciate is the *systemic* nature of mind."

DR: We contain multitudes and are part of everything. So, with Bateson, were you studying a particular subject with him, or was it more of an educational gathering forth of all-and-everything?

SN: The educational interweaving of all of life—learning to think and feel and produce. Gregory labeled himself as an anthropologist or biologist but the anthropologists never fully accepted him as an anthropologist because he was also doing biology and philosophy and natural history.

He was responsible for putting me on to William Blake, who's sort of in the same boat. Blake was a poet, painter, philosopher, and musician. He sang his own songs of Innocence and Experience. But living in the age of Guido, not Tom, he didn't know music notation, so the songs never went beyond the people who were present when he sang them. Two centuries later, I and hundreds of other people have created Blake music but we'll never know his own Blake music.

The issue for Blake, as for Bateson, for you and me and many of us who don't fit into the accepted categories, is this: Where do you file us in the library? Some of Blake is under Poetry, some under Art, some under History of Ideas, but to him, his work was one. And what about us? Do we want to put your work, David, in Philosophy or Music or Literature or Biology or Ecology or Politics? It's nonsense! Bateson taught me how to live outside of the nonsense and how to do natural history, how to pay attention to the systems of life without chopping them into little pieces.

DR: So, you learned from him how to make sense rather than nonsense?

SN: Yes! Sense is not something you can summarize or put in

a little pot and serve to people. The sense can be made only by playing together and getting into the pot and stirring it together. Gregory said that you have to get your knowledge into your elbows.

DR: I often wonder what Bateson's legacy is among the people who studied with him and have carried his ideas forward. He is so hard to categorize, but everyone who met him seems to have been deeply touched.

SN: There are quite a number of us who are writing and still hang out together. When Gregory talked about getting ideas into your body, that's one of the things that spurred me to become an improvisational musician. I became an improviser after I started working with him. It became a way of *doing* philosophy—not in the realm of words or ideas but in the realm of physical activity that you perform with your body and with sound.


## YOU HAVE TO *PERFORM* PHILOSOPHY


DR: You have to perform philosophy.

SN: There was a Zen priest who became a good friend of mine. He played tanpura on one of my records a few years later. When I first met him, he talked about sitting zazen as *practice*. Of course I'd heard that word many times before—they use it all the time, sitting meditation as *practice*. But somehow I hadn't connected it with that other something I do called music, which is also practice. I realized that music and Zen are connected; both are ways of embodying ideas. Not just cognitively, but in your elbows, as Bateson used to say.

That is where this work comes from for me: practice. Gregory died at the San Francisco Zen Center in 1980 on Independence Day. There were these black-robed Zen monks present in the corners of the room, and then he was gone and they remained. During the whole week that we were there—he was in the hospital for three weeks and then at Zen Center for one week—the monks would just sit there and do zazen in the corners of the room, breathing with him as he lay dying of respiratory disease. When something needed to be done, one of them would jump up and do it right away and be very aware of what was happening.

When he disappeared there in that room, and I found myself at Zen Center, I realized that this was the next thing I had to learn. Playing an instrument is one way of getting ideas into your body and your elbows; sitting zazen on a cushion and doing "nothing" is a way of getting philosophy into your bones.

DR: When playing music, when it's working, you get away from worrying about the activity, what it's for, or whether it's any good. You just do it. You're in it. Even when you're massaging the sound afterward, you're going toward some goal that only you hear. It's an easy way to get away from these concerns and uncertainties.

I've been very interested in Zen Buddhism and its literature, from Dōgen to *The Blue Cliff Record* and other things, but I've never felt I had the discipline to really practice Zen, which requires some severity and diligence. What I always liked about these texts is that they subvert one's sense of logic, like the John Cage idea of listening, playing, and composing having nothing to do with one another. It messes with your head but is still a precise statement. Like the buffalo that passes through a lattice window: the head, the body, the legs, all pass through, then the tail gets stuck. What is that? It's somehow against logic, but such is life.

SN: Yes, right here is a picture of that buffalo.

DR: Of course you have such a picture. Why would I expect anything else?

## WHY DOES HE ONLY PLAY IN E?

SN: I remember introducing a friend who's deeply proficient in Western music, both classical and jazz, to Indian music. I sent him some of Ram Narayan's recordings. Yehudi Menuhin thought that Ram Narayan was one of the best string players he'd ever met. His playing of ragas was as deep as it gets. He played the sarangi, an instrument with three bowed strings and thirty-eight sympathetic strings, where the *sa* as they call it in Indian music, or what we call the tonic in Western music, was always the same. My friend said, "This is such interesting music, but he always plays in E."

Other Indian musicians might play on a different *sa* from one evening to another, depending on how their instrument is tuned, but they still play on the same *sa* throughout a concert, and for Ram it was the same *sa* for his entire life. He was one of the most lucid, fluid, virtuosic improvisers around, yet from a certain Western point of view, it's always based on the same thing.

DR: You wonder what Yehudi Menuhin thought, because this guy was clearly deep in the Western tradition but he could listen outside his own tradition. This didn't bother him.

SN: Absolutely. I talked to Yehudi quite a bit about that. He was deeply interested in not only Indian music but also jazz and gypsy music. He saw the universe of variety within Ram Narayan's modal playing based on that constant E. But when Menuhin played with Ravi Shankar, he had Shankar write out the parts for him in notation. As much as he admired improvisation, he couldn't do it. He couldn't step across the corridor.

DR: Would you say that he wanted to write down even more about what's in the music, which is evidenced in that Bach score we talked about earlier?

SN: He must have wanted more on the page than the original score wanted to offer ... and in Bach's day a score was an invitation to a performer's imagination rather than the unchangeable Law.

DR: Was he just writing the exact fingerings and extra inflections? The whole thing looks like abstract art ...

SN: That page is a palimpsest in that it has layers and layers. You may keep the printed score of a piece that you've played your entire life. You notate "2" for playing a note with your second finger on this score in 1926. Then, in 1935, you decide it would be more graceful to play it with your third finger. You erase it and write a "3" over it. But the eraser isn't perfect, so the pages get messier and messier over the years, as in the case of Menuhin's manuscript. Layers and layers of these scribbles appear on top of each other. Here is this group of five notes to be tied together in one bow, but maybe later you want to tie three together followed by two singles. He seems to have been constantly changing his mind as he continued to explore this piece over his entire life. And this is just one page out of sixty.

DR: He must have wanted to see it all at once, like a child's drawing of a whole epic battle as one crazy scrawled mess, describing everything that happened and led to that point. We see so many fantastic layers of interpretation in Menuhin's one incredible image.

SN: Exactly. One of the ways in which I envy composers of notated music is this: If you and I improvise a five-minute piece of music, it takes five minutes to play and five minutes to listen to. Let's say we've accumulated a large number of pieces, as we did. Then, we try to decide what's in and what's out on the recording, or what needs to be edited a bit. If you have the music on a page, or if you have a painting on a canvas, you can do a little dab here and a little dab there and decide that the upper left-hand corner needs work and that sort of thing. You get a view like William Blake when he said, "I see past, present, and future existing all at once." I love it when you can *see* something of the sound; we get a bit of that when soundwaves are visualized on the computer. You can look at the waveform of a piece and notice a jagged spot at 2 minutes and 13.5 seconds. But it's still not the same as the painter's all-at-once overview.

DR: We do spend time composing with the sounds, making the work after it's played. You listen to it, adjust, get the sound exactly "right," using some parts and discarding others while trying to retain the improvisatory quality of the whole thing. What's always interested in me is the process of the composer who writes on the page instructions for someone else to make the music. Let's see what these instructions can make people do! And I guess that's why I've never been so happy doing it. Whenever I do, I think, "Why should I put down these notes as opposed to any others? How do I know what these musicians should do?" I can guide them in a certain way but I might as well tell them, "Just start walking left with your trombone until you hit a wall." I don't want to tell them to play *exactly* these notes. I still have this prejudice against what I'm doing, believing somewhere inside that composed music is more serious than what I am improvising.

SN: Well, that's a whole other issue. Someone is always pointing somewhere else and saying, "*That* is the real music."

DR: Is the *better* music the music that's taken longer to put together? Do we hear it in a different way? I can't hear forty-minute symphonies and understand what's happening. I feel I can sort of hear what Keith Jarrett is doing when he improvises long, unfolding pieces. I feel like he's doing something I wish other people would do more of. I know that Indian music was never interested in harmonies. When melody is explored to this level of depth, it can take many hours—even all night—to experience. We're not thinking, "Where is this melody going to go? Where is it *leading*?" You just have this melody and these rules and you go deep into them. It's a different paradigm. That's why Menuhin liked it. He never claimed he could *do* it, but he realized its significance.

SN: Exactly.

DR: I feel like I get it more than things I was studying that required me to learn about modulations and chord progressions. I never quite believed in all that.

SN: I just don't have a mind for the chord progressions. I admire people who do have that kind of mind, but it's not my

mind. The difference between me and people who have im-
poster syndrome is that I *am* an imposter.

It's also wonderful to look at Beethoven's handwriting. His
scores look a bit like Menuhin's palimpsests. His manuscripts
are so scribbly and scratchy and so much is crossed out. You
see items that popped up early in his work that got finished
twenty-five years later. Like archaeological strata. I find that
truly wonderful.


## ONLY READ THE PURPLE CLOUDS

SN: On the matter of notation; there are always *these* — [pulls
out some Rorschach inkblot cards].

DR: Graphic notation for therapy. Let's talk about something
other than your problems! It always fascinated me that people
took such things seriously, that psychologists might give us
cool shapes to talk about.

SN: I have an old friend, a flutist in L.A. named Ellen Burr.
She and I have played together for decades, and recently over
the internet as you and I have. Many years ago, she did a mu-
sical Rorschach-type project called *Ink Bops*. It is a deck of
playing cards with abstract patterns and squiggles. You in-
vent various games where you put a group of cards together
in some sequence and play them on your instrument:

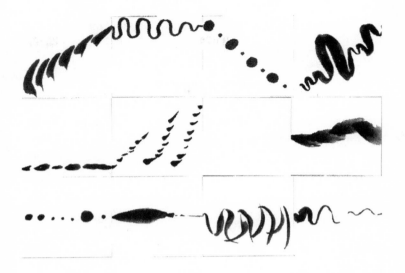

DR: That's good. So some people only play the purple cloud parts?

SN: In my workshops, I often pull out the Rorschach cards and have people play them. Or Tarot cards. If we have an all-day workshop where there's time and space to do it, I'll have people create graphic scores. We get big sheets of poster paper, two by three feet or more, and lots of watercolors and markers. People are crawling around on the floor making these wild abstract drawings for other people to play, treating the drawings as though they were recipes for music. It brings in this kindergarten energy; everybody regresses together, getting down on the floor to make these simple artworks, helping one another with their projects, and so on. Then, someone will pick up a sheet and invite two or three other people to bring their instruments over and play it. It's so much fun because it taps into being a little kid. That scribbling energy carries forward into the music that we still can make even though we are supposed to be adults.

The image isn't telling people what to do in what sequence; it's something for the performers to project their own fantasies onto. Graphic scores are a kind of halfway house between notation and improvisation. They are an expressive medium for musicians who enjoy having a recipe for music represented on a piece of paper. Going all the way means letting go of the paper and the recipe entirely and trusting that *listening*, along with *feeling* the touch of an instrument in your hands, is all you need.

DR: I wrote in a catalog essay that the rise of graphic scores in the world of contemporary music was to force classically trained musicians into improvisation when they were used to reading things as they were exactly on the page. The graphics don't tell you what to do, don't really tell you anything. In the same essay, I end with a contemporary example, the composer Matthew Burtner. I think he lives in Charlottesville. He has this whole diagram in his score of data on climate change. It's graphic notation madness. I said, "This score of yours is so beautiful." And he said, "Yes, but you should realize that this notation isn't beautiful. I had to use this notation because it is the only way to get my musicians to do what I want them to do." He is a true composer.

I brought my son to visit Harvard when he was applying to colleges. We went to the music department. It was a very interesting day to go there because there was this composition seminar for grad students led by Chaya Czernowin, a very careful and intense composer whose work involves graphic scores *and* through-written parts. All the most serious students were there, served a fancy vegan lunch before a presentation of this elite and dissonant music. Afterward, we went to Vijay Iyer's class where Wadada Leo Smith was visiting that day.

SN: Wadada is terrific! Such a warm person.

DR: He's drawing this graphic score on the blackboard, inventing the thing right there. He's so excited and says to us, "Hey, good to see you!" I hardly know him but he's being so welcoming. The class had all their instruments out, and he was creating this graphic score and just making people play it. Now, this is Harvard, so everyone had these arcane weird instruments: some strange medieval things, a hybrid gamelan creation passed down in someone's family from generation to generation, and the like. He was allowing everyone to experiment using the same tool Czernowin had used but from a very different place and with a completely different attitude.

SN: Like comedy compared to tragedy—two contrasting aspects of music using the same tool.

DR: It was such a looser mood. Czernowin was far more distant and imposing, her work suggesting, "I am the composer here." Very serious, like Stockhausen saying many years ago in a score, "Here, play in the rhythm of the universe," and musicians asked, "How will I know when I am playing in the rhythm of the universe?" "Vehl," he answered, "I will tell you."

SN: I have to be in your universe. What if I want to be in another?

DR: You wonder how the students felt about these two classes, what connected these attitudes toward music, what to make of improvisation, and how seriously to take it. I'm reminded of the opera coach Jeffrey Goldberg, one of the finest musicians I have ever known. He knows every single opera, all the scores, and he's teaching people to sing them. He knows so much of music history but he really wants to improvise. "It doesn't matter how much I know, I still have to do this." And that's a different attitude toward what one should do.

When I play on film scores, every single thing is exactly planned out—every second, every note—and I always wonder, "Why can't we just watch the scene and improvise?" That's just not how it's done. A handful of film scores are made that way, but usually not because there's this exactness to the whole process.

## CINEMA OF WONDER

SN: Speaking of film, in my opinion, the finest film that I have ever seen is *Wings of Desire* by Wim Wenders. You can't say it was quite improvised, but it's pretty close. There are these incredible long scenes, internal monologues of characters, that take up most of the movie. It's their thoughts moving in and out of the world. The monologues were sketched out after the film was recorded and they were semi-improvised.

DR: I wonder how improvised it is. That's also one of my fa-
vorite films. Wim Wenders is one of a handful of people I've
met who I was afraid to talk to. I wrote about him in my book
*Nightingales in Berlin*. I'm not sure what he thinks about what
I said about him. He lives in the apartment I lived in for one
month in Berlin while working on that project. He has my
book, in English and German. I wonder if he has read it. But,
do tell me why is this one of your favorite films. Because of its
improvised quality?

SN: Because it has a very deep heart, because it goes deep into
the human experience, deep into love, deep into the frustra-
tion of being a human being and the frustration of being a su-
pernatural being. How the humans and the angels envy each
other is just so beautiful. And, of course, Peter Handke's writ-
ing in it is so poetic, just extraordinary. Every time I see it, it
never fails to move me, even though I've seen it many times.

DR: How do you think Peter Handke's writing connected to
the improvisatory sections? Did he, in fact, write all those
parts?

SN: It certainly feels like a stream of consciousness, except it's
a stream of consciousness that just keeps going deeper and
deeper and deeper, you know? The sense of pathos and love
that comes through that film is extraordinary. It's probably
Peter Falk's greatest role: playing himself playing Columbo
the detective, shaking hands with the empty air where he
knows the angel is standing, saying, "I can't see you but I
know you're there."

DR: I have talked to Peter Handke because once I titled a record after one of his books. My record *One Dark Night I Left My Silent House*, with Marilyn Crispell, is named after his book *On a Dark Night I Left My Silent House*. I handed him a copy, and he said, "Oh, I have this. I know." There is one film he did together with Wenders where Handke directed. It's called *The Left-Handed Woman*. It's about World War Two in France. Everything's turned German, all the shops are selling German things and people are disgusted by this.

In *Nightingales in Berlin*, I wrote about how you could tell that Wenders was in love with the actress Solveig Dommartin. They were together for a while, and then she rarely acted after and died quite young.

SN: The film *Until the End of the World* was the next film that he made after *Wings of Desire* and before the sequel, *Faraway, So Close! Until the End of the World* is also quite remarkable. Solveig Dommartin is amazing in that film, and the music was one of the best compilations of pop music that ever accompanied a film. The CD of that music is extraordinary.

DR: That film also has David Darling's music in it, to whom we dedicated one of our pieces after we learned of his passing.

I've also thought about how film connects to music and improvisation. I like movies that have this improvisatory quality; they seem to go somewhere and you get surprised. I love surprise.

SN: In an interview after the film, Peter Falk, trying to describe what he was supposed to do, said, "I play an ex-angel."

One of the things about improvisation and film is that film requires a fairly large crew, even if it's not a Hollywood blockbuster. The more people to be organized and the more types of disciplines to be organized and the more budget that's organized, it's harder and harder to do anything improvisational because you have the problem of putting all the pieces together and all the people knowing what the pieces are.

There are lots of episodes of improvisation in Hollywood films, where the actor simply goes off script and improvises a scene, and it can be quite wonderful, but it's within the context of a highly structured plan. It's the same in music. For two or three or five of us to play an improvised piece, it will turn out well. But if you are interested in the sonorities of a symphony orchestra, it's very hard to get a hundred people to go off-score successfully. I've done improv workshops with a hundred people or more. They turn out very beautiful, but they aren't performances.

DR: Unless you have a piece like Terry Riley's *In C*, which is sort of improvised.

SN: With *In C* and similar pieces, you have a loose structure with scored segments. Within that structure, you can have a lot of freedom. But the more people you have playing it, the more structure you need to have just to maintain some clarity. I'd love to see gorgeous, freeform, absolutely blossoming-from-the-unconscious pure improvisation for a large orchestra. But this tends to be more the work of one person or two or five or ten people, not the work of a hundred.

DR: Or you need a very special group. What I have always

49

liked about Terry Riley's music is the improvisatory quality that sometimes you don't hear in the music of Phillip Glass or Steve Reich, although they seemed to have taken ideas from improvisatory music, from African music, from Gamelan music, from the world's repetitive musics, yet stylized them so much that it's considered more serious by *some* people. Terry Riley was always so much looser, like the West Coast itself.

SN: This is a whole other theme, the contrasting styles of East Coast/West Coast, uptown/downtown.

Say you're a downtown funky improv cellist and your friend is playing the Tchaikovsky violin concerto up at Lincoln Center. The Tchaikovsky concerto is fast and virtuosic and requires tremendous skill. In your funky setting downtown, you want to show that your playing is as fast and challenging as your friend's. I find some improvisation kind of irritating because there's no silence in it and there's no space. As I get older, I like silence and I like space. I need space in order to process sounds, to feel the consequences of each move.

DR: Another late, great improvising musician, Richard Teitelbaum, would play all these electronic sounds so quietly. Like no one else. It was an amazing thing. Just what you didn't expect from normal synthesizer music. He didn't just age into that approach, I think he did it when he was younger, too. There *is* another side to this wild improvised way of getting it all out there—the rage, the anger, the emotion, the expression that makes it more like punk or like the blues, so down to earth that if you stylize it, you call it improvisation.

Stravinsky wrote his *Three Pieces for Solo Clarinet* based on jazz. I grew up playing that before I became a jazz musician, but I think I saw from the beginning that he was reaching toward music that he didn't quite get, writing it exactly down, kind of taking something away in the process.

SN: You're taking away this raw earthiness that the angels in *Wings of Desire* don't have.

DR: You have to throw out that paradigm, think a whole different way. What if a short concert was a few hours long and that the right length was all night. That would go against everything that people are taught to believe. It's a whole different way of making sense. I'm sure you've heard this a quote from Ben Mandelson when he was in the group 3 Mustaphas 3, a pioneering world music ensemble whose motto was "Four-fifths of the world cannot be wrong."

SN: Yes, I have heard that.

DR: Four-fifths of the world is like: no harmonic movement, no modulations. The music is all based on rhythm. It's kind of improvised. Maybe it doesn't have a beginning, middle, or end. That's what most of the world's music seems to be about. Only one-fifth of the world is worried about the concerns of Western music. Maybe that's what it means.

SN: Climax structure is very interesting. In Western art—whether it be music, novels, or movies—we expect that there'll be a certain structure to time: establishment, develop-

ment, building the conflict, getting to a climax, and then re-
lease in the final moments. Life doesn't work in that novelistic
way. Most of the world's music and other art forms don't work
in that way, either. But we in the West are so interested in this
kind of story, insisting this is how it's done. Messiaen is no-
table in the Western music tradition for not having this kind
of temporal structure.

DR: Now the idea is the story should go on and on like a TV
series. Keith Jarrett's *Sun Bear Concerts* on Netflix! I've always
wondered about that assumed structure myself. It makes me
think of this Iranian film, *The Silence*, directed by Mohsen
Makhmalbaf. It's about this kid who's blind and it's filmed in
Tajikistan. His mother lost her job. They don't have any
money. The kid, who's maybe eight years old, has to go out
and work but can't see anything. He just listens. But wherever
he goes, it's so beautiful. This place, this urban Tajik environ-
ment—Dushambe, perhaps. He's listening to all the sounds.
His mother says, "You be careful on the bus because I know
what you do. You hear a beautiful sound and just follow it.
You get off the bus, but don't do that. Stay on to the end, the
last stop, you know?" And he just hears all kinds of interesting
sounds. He gets off at the wrong stop, following a sound. He
ends up at this musical instrument shop where he gets a job
tuning these wild stringed instruments, and then he goes to
where there's a whole festival of them in a park, hundreds of
people playing these *tars* or something like that. You don't
even know if it's real. It seems improbable that there would
ever be an orchestra of these things. And he's there saying,
"No, no, no, it's all out of tune." And it just goes on from there
... It's a beautiful film about listening and paying attention to

the world in a special way. I guess I'm looking for an art to something that changes the way we see the world.

SN: Exactly, exactly. *Wings of Desire* certainly has that.

## PSYCHOPOMP AND CIRCUMSTANCE

SN: The work I find the most interesting is work that functions as a psychopomp.

DR: A what?

SN: A psychopomp is a person who escorts you into another mental state.

DR: Well, this seems to be a word you did not make up. I just haven't heard of it. The pictures that come up seem to relate to *Wings of Desire*.

SN: A psychopomp is like a guide, like Virgil taking Dante through the realms of Hell, Purgatory, and Paradise. He or she is a guide to not just another land but another land of the mind, another way of seeing things and *integrating* the world. Some people who served as guides in psychedelic trips back in the day regarded themselves as psychopomps or tried to behave as such. It's a person who as a guide doesn't dictate your experience or teach you but escorts you safely to a place where you can have new experiences. Hence, the title of the album we have done together: *From This World, Another.*

At one point in my years of teaching improv workshops,

the host who was presenting me described me as an improvisation guide. I thought that was a wonderful term. Many people teach or direct improv, whether in theater or music. They like to give direction, are into theater games from Viola Spolin and others. These are wonderful activities to try, but I don't have patience for either following or giving instructions. What's fun for me is just opening the door and setting up a context where participants walk through the door and discover what they can do together. I set up these very loose things and do not tell people too much. The most successful workshops that I've taught have been workshops where I haven't said anything.

DR: Like Thich Nhat Hanh used to do, a silent retreat that would last for a week!

SN: I find I can just smile, hold hands with people, gesture. They just start making and passing around noises, and the sounds and movements begin to coalesce into coherent pieces with structure and character all their own. They start forming groups and creating interesting art. I don't have to say much.

DR: Does that work better with theater people or musicians?

SN: It can work equally well with both.

DR: What's that about, not wanting to follow instructions? I feel I'm the same way. Whenever someone wants me to do something, I want to do something else!

SN: That's why you and I are hanging out together!

DR: I don't want to follow the instructions, but other times I feel overly critical and suspicious of things that sound too random. And, as you say, I don't like loud, crazy improvisation that tries to be connected to nothing. Once, when I was playing a concert with Barry Guy, the great crazy bass player, I suggested, "Why don't we play this tune?" And he seemed kind of offended at the very idea. He must have a certain sense of entering a world where anything's possible, a world without constraints. You don't have to do everything at once, which reminds me of the philosopher Bruce Wilshire, who used the phrase "the much-at-once."

SN: The Emperor said to Mozart, "Too many notes, too many notes!"

DR: Everyone plays fewer notes when they get older. I remember talking to Steve Gorn after he had a stroke and got better. He said, "You just can't play all those notes." It was kind of a corrective for him.

SN: That's why I didn't like Morton Feldman when I was thirty-five. But now that I'm seventy, I love his music.

DR: It's good that we're not fixed in our opinions.


## RAVI SHANKAR'S POODLE


SN: About two years before he died, Ravi Shankar came here to Charlottesville with his daughter Anoushka and played a concert. He was already ninety and she's the virtuoso now. He was the dazzling virtuoso when he was younger, and now he would just play single tones to reverberate through your bones, and they would just completely shake you. It was just one tone, then another tone, and then another. It was clear that he still *did* have the chops to play fast and furious, but he was in another place.

DR: Did they get along musically?

SN: Extremely well. The love of guru and student, parent and child, was palpable. She is in her own unique realm as an artist. I spent some time with him after the concert. The first thing that he asked me when I walked in the room was, "Do you have a dog?"

DR: What did you say?

SN: I said, "No, I'm allergic now. But I adore dogs and I used to have them and I love them." His poodle was with him throughout the concert, on the stage.

DR: Did he ever play without the poodle?

SN: Of course, but he trained the poodle to be especially well behaved, to be part of the show. And the dog was sitting at his feet in the room where we were talking.

DR: Interesting.

SN: It was great to watch that settled quality he had. There's something interesting about age. I love the final album of Leonard Cohen, *You Want It Darker*. There's something about being old and slow and having that gravelly voice.

DR: He got better. His voice improved with age. Totally changed. A very good argument for smoking.

SN: That's okay. I think I'll pass.

Yesterday I spoke with a woman named Briony Greenhill, an English singer and vocal improviser who is now in France. We were talking about this whole business, and I told her about what you and I were doing over the internet and the problem of latency—or the non-problem of latency. She came up with this wonderful term: "seaweed time." Musicians have been conditioned to the beat and the bar. They play with software like Ableton, which makes the unexamined assumption that all music is structured in terms of beats and bars.

Early in the pandemic I did an experiment with four singers in L.A. where we just tried clapping, playing over Zoom, trying to see if we could do synchronized beats. Of course, it was way off. Not only that, but it was way off in a different way for each of the people on the screen. We all heard the claps in different sequences. But when you and I have played together over the internet, and when I've played with other people and we're just *with* each other and playing through this gulf of time, space, and electronics, it works out perfectly. The pulse of the music transcends beats and bars. It feels connected, and time as we experience it is fine.

That's what Greenhill meant about the seaweed structure of time—that time is not grids and bars. It's just seaweed, waving back and forth in the water.

DR: I heard an interview with the young prodigy Jacob Collier, who automatically plays out of sync to make sure it sounds in sync with the other musician. I guess he feels he's petrified the seaweed.

When I teach students how to use Ableton Live, I always tell them to turn off the quantization, the bar lines, and the snap-to-grid function because music, like the world, is not in these grids. Keep them on if you need them sometimes, but then you have to transcend them. Don't let them rule you.

SN: It's pretty interesting how people want to get stuck. They assume that technology needs these things. It's the same with intonation as well. We've talked about the idea that the beat kept should never be too regular. It has to be a little bit off. Just when you think it's not quite right, you probably should keep it there. Keep listening. Real people are never as exact as their machines.

We have these unexamined assumptions that life accords itself to the machines that we have in our culture. This was certainly true in science in the eighteenth century, when they had the idea of the clockwork universe. William Paley, a hundred years before Darwin, was already defending orthodox Christianity against the idea of evolution by coming up with this idea of intelligent design—that you look at your watch and your watch was designed for a purpose, so it must have had a designer. Therefore, the universe is like this. In the nineteenth century, we had Freud's model of the unconscious as a steam engine with pressure and pipes and release valves and so on. Later, we had ideas of mechanisms like the telegraph as a model for the mind, and now it's the computer. Science reporters will constantly say, "The brain is a computer and it does dah, dah, dah." We reflexively look at the devices that we've created and we think these devices are the model for how the living biological universe works. But the biological universe is a billion times older than these machines.

DR: We are too impressed by the things we use every day. And they're used as models for things that we never made, that no one made, that nobody understands.

SN: I was outdoors yesterday recording woodpecker sounds. It's wonderful how much a woodpecker sounds like a bass drum if you drop it four octaves. Then you can hear how the drumbeat of each burst of pecks is constantly slowing down. The woodpecker doesn't have a metronomic beat. These are the rhythms of nature. Not a grid. Not a clock.

DR: One of the best things one can do in learning from natural sounds is to take them and transform them using technology into something we can hear and make some sense of. Through that process, we learn from nature. If it's irregular, you stick with it. Go with that irregularity, take it in, and say, "Okay, that's what *this* does. Let's just use it."

SN: Always asking what we can we learn from nature.

DR: When I teach people to work with sounds that are unfamiliar, I say, "Learn from the sound, change your music because of this." In other words, don't just stick it in the familiar box where it becomes just an addition to what you were doing. Have the experience and the source change *you*. Due to my questioning philosophical side, which is what can easily prevent someone from believing full steam in what they're doing, I still wonder, "Why is it that I like improvisation more than composition? Like, who am I kidding? What's so great about making stuff up as you go along?" I might have a bias toward the unknown or wanting to be surprised.

SN: I would hope so! Biased toward the unknown—that's synonymous with the word *learning*.

## YOU CANNOT REHEARSE FOR THE UNKNOWN

DR: There's a Wayne Shorter film, *The Language of the Unknown*, where his group is in the huge, fancy auditorium of the Cité de la Musique in Paris. They're announcing one of his famous tunes like "Footprints" and they play. They take off in a direction that has hardly anything to do with the tune. Complete free improvisation. The audience is in rapt attention. They know they're experiencing something special that can't be written down. Then, in the film, they're just listening to the recording afterward and you see Wayne's face as he's listening to certain things that go on, reacting with subtle smiles and laughs—such joy and attention as he follows along with his own thought process.

SN: Joy in attention, to my mind, comes from surprise. There's a certain pleasure of surprise that we experience. You and I share a certain personality type who tends to like this. Whereas a great musician like Leonard Bernstein might conduct Mahler's Second Symphony for the eighty-fifth time. He does it with interpretive variations, but it's recognizably the same piece every one of those eighty-five times. He's in such ecstasy with those sounds and bringing a sense of communion together among the musicians. While I so enjoy hearing music I've heard many times before, what excites me is a moment in which somebody says something or there's a musical sound in a film that is truly new. It might be very simple; it doesn't have to be fancy or elaborate but it stands out and stops you in your tracks. That's what's exciting to me. And that's why I love improvising.

DR: He wanted to make it ecstatic. He was showing you that it was possible to be emotional about this. His music was full of this quality and he wasn't afraid to reveal that. I don't know what he thought about improvisation. I think he was a complicated character, but I imagine he probably spent a lot of time just jamming with people.

He was an amazing figure. We don't have anyone quite like that now, nor could we, given the way the world is now. The world of jazz improvisation, with great individual figures with a particular sound, is not really in the discourse these days.


## MESSIAEN AND PLAYING WITH BIRDS


SN: Olivier Messiaen is a wonderful ancestor to invoke in this work. Composers have been connecting with birdsong for thousands of years. But he pioneered a more intimate, interesting connection with birdsong. His connection of nature with spirituality was extraordinary, and his mastery of orchestral sound enabled him to portray birdsong with ordinary instruments. His magical timbres, the mergings and the clashings of sounds in his music, are astonishing. In my book *The Art of Is*, I evoke *thinking as nature thinks* as a hallmark of creativity. Messiaen certainly knew how to think as nature thinks and bent the rules of music accordingly.

We are part of this ancient and still-ongoing stream of musicians who have been inspired by birds. Thanks to recording technology, we can improvise-compose-improvise-compose in concert with them in ways that were not possible before. One of my oldest improv companions, Ron Fein, just came out with his own album of bird music. It's called *Equatorial*. He made it entirely out of recordings from the xeno-canto archive, using birds that live right on the equator. It is a journey all the way around the equator through the processed voices of those birds.

DR: Xeno-canto is one of the positive things about the internet. It's this incredible resource of user-uploaded birdsongs from everywhere in the world. It has high-quality geo-located recordings. You can download and use them. Previously, this stuff was all hidden behind expensive institutions. The world is changing in that sense.

SN: I'm doing some experiments now using some of these archives. In my last album, *Hermitage of Thrushes*, I used only the birds that I had personally recorded within walking distance of my house.

Now that spring is just about to pop, I'm looking forward to making more recordings of the local birds, but there's a gigantic universe beyond that. I'm starting to work with some of those exotic animal sounds that other people have recorded.

DR: Xeno-canto is an amazing source for those. Some of the most interesting songs are restricted because there's birds like the shama thrush from India that people illegally send around the world. Those are blocked on xeno-canto, interestingly enough.

SN: Why is it illegal?

DR: They don't want to encourage traffic in illegal species around the world. Some of these super-singers are among them.

SN: They're concerned that people will come and try to hunt them.

DR: They play recordings of those sounds to lure and capture them, then whisk them out of the country. Other people are concerned you're going to play these songs and mess up the local birds by teaching them weird stuff, which I think is only a positive development. Still, what amazes me is how much we don't know about most birdsongs.

SN: If we don't trash the entire planet, there's so much we can still discover.

# Listening to the pieces

## 1) FLY, SING, DREAM: NIGUNIM AND ROBIN-CHAT

SN: Let's begin with the first piece: "Fly, Sing, Dream." I love the way the birds in these pieces kind of blurred the personalities. When I'm playing violin or you're playing clarinet, it's clear who's who, but when I'm playing birds or when you're playing birds, it's not clear who's who.

DR: You mean our personalities don't come through in the birds that we play? I think they do.

SN: Maybe they do, but not in a way that's obvious to the listener.

DR: I feel like you're playing with this recording of a bird. I believe it is a white-throated robin-chat.

SN: This one is your bird.

DR: Yes, it *was* the white-throated robin-chat, and then we heard the blue rock thrush. Olivier Messiaen did such interesting things with this bird. That was the second bird that came in briefly. We'll hear more of him later.

I tried to pick birds I had not used too many times before because there are hundreds of possible birds with amazing songs. I have a lot of these recordings stored away but don't use them much. I went to something with potential I hadn't thought about. I usually take out the noise, slow it down, put the pitch down into something we could work with. And then we let it play.

SN: I do pretty much the same processing with my bird recordings. By lowering the pitch and slowing them down, we make birdsongs more accessible to the grosser sensibilities of human hearing.

I love what the birds bring to this game. Hence, this album's title: *From This World, Another*. The voices of other species bring another world into this music. It's a partnership between the two of us but it's also a partnership between us and nature, between us and this place and time and context.

As the piece progresses, I'm playing this Chinese lithophone. I'm not sure what it's called. The closest that has a name is called a *bianqing*. The tone bars are made of stone, all of them inscribed. A *bianqing* has L-shaped stones; these are straight. In this music, we're always kind of playing on the edge of the unknown—it's not always clear who's who or what's what—and we're inviting the listener into that same territory of the unknown.

DR: And now we're playing something like the wordless chants of our ancestors called the *Nigun*, which my father was always reminding me about. "Your ancestors made this music!" It's like what you do, they're going ...

SN & DR: *lai de de dai dai dai dede dai dai ...*

DR: ... all together, keep going! It's a thrumming all-around sound, and the bird encouraged us to go in that direction.

SN: When you mention Nigun, it brings up something I discovered recently that wish I had put into *The Art of Is* but didn't know then. In the chapter "Universal Language" (which used to be called "Gibberish: The Universal Language"), I talk about scat. It starts from my practice singing gibberish with people whenever I teach. I write about scat and how it began with Louis Armstrong and/or Gene Green singing songs whose words they forgot, so they made up the language on the spot. And then, on the next page, I talk about growing up Jewish in Los Angeles at this conservative synagogue, where the adults were davening and singing with great intensity in this language that to them was gibberish because they didn't know Hebrew. They just learned how to pronounce the syllables. When I was a kid, I thought this was the silliest thing I ever saw. But when I became an improviser as an adult, I realized this was one of the roots of everything I do. And I recently discovered that Louis Armstrong attributed the invention of scat to Jewish davening.

DR: Well, he knew who his friends were.

SN: He sure did. He told Cab Calloway that listening to Jews davening, he realized that this was a form of musical expression that can spread all over the world in a different form, but he didn't want to publicly attribute that because he was afraid that people think he was making fun of Jews. The origin of scat and davening and Nigun are tied up together.

SN: A lot of what we're discovering are the in-between things: in-between cultures, in-between species, in-between improvising and composing. They can't be categorized and don't fall in the silos.

DR: Listening to our first piece, it sounded very composed to me. It was totally organized. The robin-chat introduces the music and you're interacting with it, but we still hear the bird clearly. You play along with it and I join in and we kind of ecstatically go to this moment from our heritage of ancient chanting. And then, at the end, this other bird comes in; it's scratchier and noisier. It's like we've gone through the exercise necessary to understand this new confusing bird. And then it goes on to its conclusion.

## 2) AUKURAS: DESIGNER-OUT-OF-TUNE

SN: Speaking of things that don't fall in the silos, here's the next piece we're about to play. The piece is now called "Auku-ras," which is Lithuanian for a fire ritual (but we didn't know that then, as the piece was created weeks before it was named). When we recorded it together, I thought I was playing a treble viol. But I've since talked to a friend who's an expert in instruments of that period. She thinks that it's a viola d'amore without sympathetic strings. In reality it's a hybrid instrument. It doesn't need to have a name to sound good or to feel good in the hand.

DR: Where did you get it?

SN: I got it at a musical instrument auction. I've been fasci-nated by the viola d'amore and other early string instruments for a long time, especially instruments with sympathetic strings. If you've been brought up on orchestral music or pop music or whatever, you think the string family is violin, viola, cello, bass. But there are hundreds of instruments that have been invented, whether three hundred years ago or right now, that don't fall into those categories. They use many of those design principles but differently in terms of shape, size, architectural ideas, and extra strings. The idea of sympathetic strings was imported from India back in the sixteenth century. A cross-cultural hybrid, like so many of the themes we're talking about. Because I was playing with this very resonant instrument, I was going into a lot of ricochet sounds that give it room to resonate.

DR: I have a whole story about this piece. I told you I wanted to cut it because I'm playing totally out of tune. And you said, no, no, it's okay. It's like "designer-out-of-tune." I think it's a phrase I heard in Scotland once. I was so upset about being out of tune with what I thought was a viola. Now I realize you're not playing a viola but this other odd instrument. Of course, it might be tuned differently because it's not some standard thing. I was so worried about it because I know how easy it is to play these low clarinets out of tune. Listening to it now, it doesn't bother me at all.

SN: Right.

DR: And it reminded me ... we named it something Lithuanian and I have a Lithuanian folk clarinet called the *birbyne*, which, if you play the open notes on it in a scale, like on a flute or a recorder, it's this totally weird scale. To play a tempered scale, you have to use weird fingerings. Once I took it out to play with this Lithuanian folk singer, Indrė Jurgelevičiūtė, and started playing these weird notes. Instantly, she joined in with a song that was completely together with this, which I thought was out of tune but was totally in this other kind of music. Hearing the piece now, it's like, okay, now I understand why it all makes sense.

SN: It works! One thing that's fascinated me for decades is just intonation and world music scales and non-equal-tempered tuning. I wrote a piece of software in the late 1980s that actually sold and made money in the nineties called *The World Music Menu*, which allowed you to retune your synthesizer into scales from all over the world: ancient Greek scales, Indian scales, Mesopotamian scales, African scales, and so on. In the West, we've become fixated on those twelve chromatic tones because the piano is tuned that way and guitar frets are placed in those locations. We tend to think "out of tune" when we hear all those tones that are someplace else among the infinitely many stopping places between zero and one.

On a violin or cello, you can just slide up and down and place your pitches anywhere. They're essentially *analog* and allow you to play in all kinds of different intonations. One of the reasons I became fascinated by instruments with sympathetic strings is that they enable you to tune up non-standard intonations on the sympathetic strings. And then, when you're slithering and sliding around on the fingerboard of the viola d'amore or whatever instrument it is, you're getting a special resonance at those particular pitches.

The whole one-size-fits-all idea of musical pitch is an artifact of the Industrial Revolution. You can do extraordinary things on the piano thanks to those fixed equal-tempered pitches, but you are also missing out on something. In Western music, we have the ability to modulate from key to key to key, which depends on equal temperament, but we've also lost something along the way.

DR: How would you describe most succinctly what it is we have lost?

SN: Before the Industrial Revolution, if I were rich enough to have someone make a shirt for me, they would measure my body and make a shirt for me. That still happens occasionally. But now I go to the store and buy a shirt with a collar that's 15 or 15½ or 16 or 16½. This makes it possible to sell and distribute shirts in a way that wasn't possible before. But the shirt will not truly fit *me*; it's a generic item. It's the same thing musically in terms of having those fixed keys on the piano keyboard—A, B flat, B, C, C sharp, and so on—but nothing in the spaces between them.

We talked earlier about Guido of Arezzo. The huge advantage of Guido's digital communication of named notes is that you can notate them compactly and you can transport the notation easily. This was as true in centuries past as it is now. Sometimes, I'll go into a classroom full of young musicians and ask, "How many of you play notes on your instrument?" Most raise their hands. But they don't play notes on the instrument. They play tones. A T-O-N-E is a sound; an N-O-T-E is a black dot on a piece of paper. Those are two different things. They're certainly related but they're not the same thing.

What I'm interested in sonically is all those infinitely many sounds that don't fall on the predetermined grid that our culture has settled on. This is why the music of other species is so interesting.

DR: Yes. And, of course, once you spend time listening to pure intonation and other systems, it's hard to go back, you hear everything as being a little out of tune. The whole system of equal temperament is a kind of designer-out-of-tune.

SN: It's a designer-out-of-tune thing based on the square root of two, which is an irrational number. You don't have to be into the exotic knowledge of this stuff in order to do it. All you have to do is put on the Beatles' masterpiece *Sergeant Pepper's Lonely Hearts Club Band* and hear the Beatles singing in perfect just intonation relative to each other. They didn't know about all this historical mathematical stuff. They just listened to each other and sang in tune, in just intonation intervals with each other. And that's why, sort of like in Gregorian chant, their singing together sounds so exquisite.

DR: I didn't know that. But, of course, it's why people like the blue notes in between major and minor. There's something right about that. The system doesn't encompass that but we hear it and we feel it.

SN: Blues is based on ratios of seven. In the ancient Greek source of our Western system, there's the octave, which is a 2:1 ratio, meaning this tone wiggles exactly twice as fast as the lower tone. And so, they slide into the ear and sound like they fit together. What we call the perfect fifth is the 3:2 ratio in which three vibrations from one sound equals two vibrations for another, and they nicely slide into your ear. The perfect fourth is a 4:3 ratio. All of our Western scales grew out of ratios of two, three, four, and five. But the blues is ratios of seven, which exist in African music but not in European and American music. The blues third is a ratio of seven to five, which is seven vibrations to five. People with the right instruments and voices accustomed to those tones just do it naturally and instinctively without conceptualizing the math.

DR: I always thought it was a simpler ratio than the major third or the minor third. Is that true?

SN: The blues third is partway between the minor third and major second. It's a little bit smaller than a minor third. Jazz pianists do this thing called crushing where they sort of bash on the black key and their finger slips onto the white key next to it. They're giving a kind of hybrid of the two keys in order to simulate the feeling of playing partway between the two. With African instruments and African voices, they just do it naturally. It's in their elbows as Gregory Bateson liked to say.

DR: Should we listen to another one?

## 3) FOR DAVID DARLING: TALES FOR ALL PEOPLE

SN: Number three is called "For David Darling." David recently passed away and was a great guy, a great cellist, and a great teacher of improvisational music. We spoke of sympathetic vibrations in the previous piece before when I was playing a viola d'amore. In "For David Darling," I'm just plucking on an electric violin but I have a sympathetic strings effect on it. Sympathetic vibrations in those harmonic ratios are happening around those plucks.

DR: What is the effect exactly?

SN: It's a sympathetic strings effect called Superchord, which I recommend.

DR: The bird you hear there is a rufous-throated solitaire, which is a common Caribbean bird. It makes this distinct little gesture, a self-contained sound. And then, in various places, I change the pitch or do different things to it. It's like a simple song that can be messed with. You had some other effect on there, too, right?

SN: No, it was just the sympathetic string effect ...

DR: What about the *wow wow wow wow*?

SN: In the first half, I was plucking the strings; in the second half, I was playing *col legno*, which is hitting the strings with the stick of the bow. I would never do that with a nice old wooden bow. But I was playing with a carbon fiber bow, so it's fine to strike the strings with the hard part and get this metallic percussive sound.

DR: So that's an acoustic effect.

SN: An acoustic effect filtered through the electronic effect of sympathetic strings.

DR: Fascinating.

SN: It was turning the violin strings into a percussion instrument by hitting them.

DR: We wanted to dedicate something to David Darling because he meant so much to both of us. He was probably the first improvising cellist I heard as a teenager when he was playing with Paul Winter. This guy was just doing wild stuff. He was singing, he was plucking the cello. He was playing something like the blues on it, showing the possibilities of what you could do. I went to some workshops he did and met him many times over the years.

SN: He was a true human being.

DR: He started an organization to spread music and improvisation to everyone. He really wanted to get this music out.

SN: That's right, Music for People. It's still going strong and they're doing great things.

DR: I always admire these musicians who forge their own path. He didn't do regular jazz. He wasn't afraid to be bluesy sometimes and sing while playing. There was an epic depth to his cellistic chords. Sometimes, it was even guitaristic. He sort of pioneered this notion that the cello can be the whole source.

SN: Hearing you describe him as one of those musicians who created his own path made me think again of William Blake, who said, "I must create my own system." Some musicians like David, like you and me, or like many other people we know, live in a paradox. That is, we create our own systems but we're not creating our systems in a vacuum; we're creating our systems in a social universe where we're friends with other people who've also created their own systems. One of the advantages of the conventions of straight-ahead jazz or straight-ahead classical music is that people who haven't played together before can get together and sit with the notation and produce something coherent. What's interesting is that in our world of people who don't work with notation and have created all their own idiosyncratic weird systems are still able to sit down together and play and communicate across those idiosyncratic systems. It's quite beautiful.

DR: It is. You have to kind of believe that music can be made to be coherent. I know a lot of people I've worked with do not feel that way. Either they wanted to have a beginning, middle, and end or they see it all as a precise atmospheric effect. Normally you can't do film music like what we're doing. Everything is programmed, every minute, every second. There's a handful of directors who say let's improvise the music. And I think that often leads to better results. But the mainstream is absolute careful planning of every moment. Surprises should happen!

SN: While I have great admiration for my fellow musicians who are able to map out and be mapped by meticulous scores, by temperament I'm just not that sort of person. It's not a matter of better or worse. It's simply that this is what we enjoy doing. Part of the paradox of this work, as you remarked before about our first piece, is that it sounded composed. And all of these pieces we've done are coherent pieces of music. They *do* have beginnings, middles, and ends. They *do* revolve around a fulcrum. All of those structural things exist in spontaneous conversation.

DR: Structure comes by way of many methods. If you believe in improvisation, which not everyone does, you believe that people getting together and making music with a sense of the unknown brings you the most important things in music. I think it was in our podcast that I quoted the Wayne Shorter film that I liked where Danilo Pérez comes in. He's nervous. It's his first day rehearsing with Wayne. He studied every possible tune from the Wayne shorter songbook. He shows up and says, "Maestro, is there any particular selection you'd like to begin with?" "No, no, Danilo, no, no. *You cannot rehearse for the unknown.*" If you watch the film and listen to the album and these recent Wayne Shorter releases, they claim to be playing his famous, beautiful jazz compositions. There's barely a glimmer of any of them; they are not played at all. They're just *going.* They're playing free improvisation for thousands of people. And everyone knows that they're at the edge of something.

SN: It all flows together as a structure. You don't need the pre-planning to be a structure because the pre-planning is within us; the three-and-a-half billion years of activity that made us living organisms contain a lot of structure.

On this theme of improvising a piece that sounds as though it were composed, the night I was speaking with Yehudi Menuhin, when he told me to write the book that became *Free Play*, he said, write about improvisation, write about what you do. I had told him earlier about a concert that I did in Berkeley when I was first improvising. I'd been invited to an academic venue where people didn't have an idea of improvised music. Such a thing was beneath contempt. So I wrote up a fake program (which, unfortunately, I didn't save), stating that there would be four pieces.

I gave them titles and ascribed them to four obscure contemporary composers who were actually the names of four small children I knew. These children were friends who happened to be around four years old at the time. Then, I improvised four pieces. People liked the music and asked where they could find more music by these composers. I told Yehudi this story. He said, "Well, you should write a book about improvisation and call it *The Four Greatest Composers Who Ever Lived*."

DR: That's good.

SN: That was the working title of *Free Play* for about the first six years that I was writing it. Then, it became *Improvisation in Life and Art*, and finally *Free Play*.

DR: That approach worked for the artist Theaster Gates. At first, he was doing pottery, which nobody cared about—just another guy making pots. Then, he picked a different angle by claiming to have learned this pottery technique from a Japanese master living in the hills. Gates even brought him to the opening, but it was all made up. There was no master; he just hired someone to play the part of one. And then, this was heralded as the great debut of a fantastic conceptual artist who was reexamining our whole sense of creativity.

People need to be shaken up and surprised. Just like the old joke that you never shake hands with the musicians on the bandstand when you got the gig because the audience doesn't realize musicians might not know each other and yet be able to make music together.

## 4) BAMBUTA: WHOSE BIRD, YOURS OR MINE?

SN: The next piece is short: "Bambuta."

DR: And why is it called that?

SN: It's called that because my dear friend, the conductor Larry Livingston, suggested that name. It doesn't necessarily have any meaning other than Bambuta.

DR: It's a sound that came to him?

SN: It's the sound that came to him. The other day I was talking to a friend on Zoom and when we said goodbye, I said, "Hasta la Zungos!" She then emailed me quizzically, asking, "What does Hasta la Zungos mean?" I said it means goodbye for people who don't speak Spanish. So here's Bambuta.

DR: I looked up this word: Bambuta. It is a place in Liberia. We're set. Nobody's used it. I was trying to remember whose bird was played there, yours or mine. What do you think?

SN: It was your bird. I was playing violin, which needs both hands. I don't think I was pushing buttons on the side.

DR: It's the beginning of the white-throated robin-chat. I was playing this bass overtone flute, this bent piece of plastic pipe, a kind of Scandinavian instrument, a *seljefløyte* made by Jean-

Pierre Yvert, a French enthusiast of Scandinavian music. There are not too many of these instruments left anymore. They're prized as sounding better than the wooden ones. This, again, is a natural-intonation instrument that can be hard to tune with other things, but you seem to have figured it out. What were you playing there?

SN: I was playing a violin.

DR: The overtone flute gets you into this natural harmonic series. And so, I think the name fits somehow because there's nothing made of bamboo that we were playing

SN: That's right. And there's nothing made of *ta* either.


## 5) MALŪMA: THE BOUBOU/KIKI EFFECT

SN: Well, on to "Malūma." This title comes from Wolfgang Köhler, who was a pioneer of gestalt psychology in the 1920s. He did an experiment which then got replicated all over the world in innumerable cultures in innumerable languages, where he drew one figure that was all wiggling curves and a second figure that was spiky and angular.

He said to participants in the experiment, "One of these is called Takete and the other is called Malūma. Which one is which?" Virtually everybody answered the same because the visual and the auditory are connected and you don't need any training to know that. You don't need to be a native speaker of English or Swahili or live in Papua New Guinea or Scandinavia to know that. Everybody knows it because patterns are universal at that level. So that's Malūma and Takete.

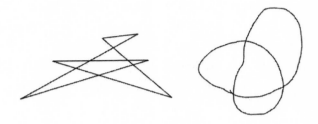

Qual è MALUMA e qual è TAKETE?

DR: I remember reading all these books when I was in living in Norway, studying with the philosopher Arne Naess, and thinking that gestalt psychology had to be a great area to investigate, the shapes and patterns of the universe. I wanted to know about these. People have told me all this stuff is wildly unpopular now. You're here fifty years too late!

SN: It can come back because it's still true.

DR: I particularly liked your voice along with the keyboard, playing these airy sounds that are, as we mentioned earlier, very Malūma. I played with this big Roland Fantom-X7 keyboard. At the time I got it, I spent a lot of time programming these sounds. It has this aftertouch where you just hold down the note and it's made out of four separate sounds. One of them changes totally when you press harder. I wouldn't remember how to program it today.

And I made my 64 favorite sounds. They're all odd world-musicky things. I'm not sure what I made them for, but as

soon as I heard one, I realized, "Oh, I want it to play this."
With the world of computers today, with all the precision you
have adjusting everything, it's much harder to play these
things. With this instrument, you just turned it on and played
it. It was very interesting hearing that mix. It sounded not just
like a droning chord on a typical synthesizer but something
being played in this odd way. People are still trying to make
electronic instruments more expressive by coming up with
new controllers.

SN: Yes, the MPE controllers we're playing with now, with
rubbery keys that you can glide your fingers across.

DR: There's something about the hardware instrument ... I've
been ignoring it for a long time but it makes sense.

SN: Speaking of non-equal-tempered instruments, the per-
cussion instrument I was playing was this Balinese metallo-
phone. The closest named instrument is called a *gendèr*. Like
all things in Balinese music, it's not equal-tempered; it's in a
Pelog scale, much beloved by Lou Harrison. A lot of the things
that we've been exploring in this album involve laying differ-
ent kinds of intonation on top of each other and finding all of
these fascinating combinations.

DR: This piece has a little bit of the sound of one of my favor-
ite groups, which was Codona with Collin Walcott, Don
Cherry, and Naná Vasconcelos.

SN: Yes, I knew Collin.

DR: He was a great character. And that group, it's very hard to emulate what they did. In fact, I've never been able to do anything close to that except with you. To put these very simple sounds together and make it work. Don Cherry could pick up anything and make it sound good, make it his own ... something I always aspired to do. Sometimes, people whined about his trumpet playing, saying this guy can't really play, but he played his own way. He would make these things work, and combining them with these two characters was very special.


## 6) GRAVITY'S WAVE: WHAT IS TIME?

SN: The next piece is called "Gravity's Wave." I was thinking of calling it "Center of Gravity" because it is the middle piece in the album. It's the longest piece of the album and is the fulcrum around which the whole thing turns. You changed it to "Gravity's Wave," which is very cool because the thing that unifies the two ends of the fulcrum is this kind of thumping ostinato in the synthesizer that sounds like the undertone of the universe. It's a mesh of multiple worlds: you're playing the synthesizer, I'm playing the *uirapuru*, this bird from the Brazilian jungle. We were talking about innovative cellists like David Darling before. A friend of mine, Pedro de Alcantara, a fabulously inventive Brazilian cellist who lives in Paris, wrote to me after I published my album *Hermitage of Thrushes* to introduce me to the uirapuru, sometimes called the musician wren. Messiaen also used the uirapuru in his 1964 piece, *Et Exspecto Resurrectionem Mortuorum*. Indigenous Amazonian people believe that the song of the uirapuru is heard by all humans at the moment of our death, so it had spiritual/mystical overtones for Messiaen. The uirapuru songs always seem to cadence with a rising fourth.

I put this bird into the first part of the piece while you were playing. The piece itself has a center of gravity because it starts with your clarinet solo and my bird and ends with my violin solo and your bird. It flips around in the middle. The piece feels very subterranean or jungle-like.

DR: I can feel all the effort we put into it to get it to work. On the one hand, you have the uirapuru, the musician wren, the most clearly tonal of the sounds here. Then we have this machine doing what machines do best, which is to repeat something over and over again. The other thing I hear in the beginning is what I love about Ethiopian rock 'n' roll and pop music: that the tritone is a consonance. It just goes on for like 10 minutes. And then, you say, okay, that's not dissonance. That's just the way the world is. We're playing with it in different ways. I'm trying to keep this tritone quality, my thinking of this Ethiopian stuff, going against the machine. And then you play this lyrical solo and the rhythm gets more subtle. That's where that bird enters from Arizona, the curve-billed thrasher song, heavily transformed and played. Every few beats I'm changing the pitch of it, so it's being *played* in the background. It's not so loud.

The repeating electronic sound is made with this software synthesizer called Alchemy that mirrors what the Fantom-X7 does—each instrument based on a mix of four different sounds. You can morph through the different sounds on the computer a little more easily than with the Fantom. Later, we tried to make sure the track had this punchiness.

SN: There was a certain prickle component, as I feel it, in the synth line and I wanted more of that to mix in.

DR: Right. And it was easy to go back and put that in. But what do you mean by a "prickle"?

SN: The thing that sounded like thousands of little steel needles making their way through the universe!

The interesting thing about that synthesizer sound is that on the one hand, it has this wave component, which is kind of Maluma. And then there's this prickle component, which is Takete. The sound of this ostinato has a mixture of Maluma and Takete. I think that's what makes it so interesting.

DR: I wonder where Wolfgang Köhler got that phrase from?

SN: When I first read about this, I was an undergraduate student at Harvard. I told an anthropologist friend of mine about it and he said that in the Fijian language they have the words *maluma* and *takelo*, which simply mean "soft" and "hard." Takete may be a word in one of the Polynesian languages.

DR: I'm reading here that after Köhler, someone named this the "Bouba/Kiki effect." There's even a video game named after this phenomenon, with the kind of title we would both want to use for an album. The title of the game is: *Baba is You.*

SN: I love the way this piece flips over. On top of this layer of Malūma/Takete that feels like gravitational waves, we've got your solo at the beginning, my solo at the end, and the place in the middle where we meet. It feels like a structure that flips over and meets itself. It's a long piece, the pivot point of the whole album.

DR: What is long? What is short? What is time?

This piece is in the middle and the name, of course, alludes to gravitational waves, the earliest sounds in the universe. Imagine the vast effort it took to discover that sound, which is like building these long tunnels above the ground, in the desert, in different parts of the world. And they're trying to record something like a sound beyond sound. It's like a metaphor for the beginning of all noise and everything else.

## 7) BEAUTIFUL EGGS: THE JUNGLE AT NIGHT

SN: One of the things that I liked when we were putting this album together is the sequence of "Gravity's Wave" transitioning into "Beautiful Eggs." Of course, it wasn't called "Beautiful Eggs" then.

DR: This isn't the actual order in which we played the pieces.

SN: It just happened on our first run through possible sequences that those two were next to each other. And I loved that. We both thought of tunnels in describing what had yet to be called "Gravity's Wave." You're traversing some kind of mysterious subterranean tunnel or a tunnel through the desert, or I think of it as a tunnel through the jungle, because of the bird. And then you come out of the tunnel and suddenly you're in this vast open place that clearly feels like a forest at night; it's very alive and very open. There is a sense that a door has been opened and now we're in this vast nighttime space.

I love that transition.

DR: Nice. Now I remember where the title comes from. We were reading about mockingbirds. We went to the classic early twentieth-century compendium of bird lore by Arthur Cleveland Bent to see what could be said about the mockingbird. The thing we noticed in this long account about the bird was it has beautiful eggs!

SN: That's right. I recorded this mockingbird in my neighbor's tree.

DR: Yes. It had this local in-the-place quality.

SN: My neighbor was complaining about this bird. He told me that he was glad something musically good came of it. He and his wife are driven crazy by this mockingbird, who sings all night in their tree.

DR: When are we going to shoot him?

SN: Exactly.

DR: As I was listening to this piece, I thought you were playing this pizzicato on the violin. Were you?

SN: Yes.

DR: And then I started playing a whole mixture of odd electronic synth sounds, just letting loose on this keyboard. Oh, it could do *this*! It could do *that*! But I was trying to make that not overwhelm. As someone who's not usually playing those kinds of sounds, it was an interesting test.

SN: On this one and "For David Darling," I am playing all pizzicato. I usually don't do that. That was a lot of fun for me.

DR: So many ways to play these instruments! And the mockingbird! We might've talked elsewhere about how I'm currently working on a science paper with these two different kinds of scientists trying to decode the song of the mockingbird. It's fifty pages and includes ten detailed diagrams. One person is the world expert on hearing what a mockingbird is doing; he can identify everything that's happening. The other is a computational neuroscientist; she can back up our hypotheses by crunching all the numbers. I add the musical perspective. The reviewers of this paper for the journal constantly complained about everything we're doing, but eventually they had to accept it—we just had too much data and analysis for them to reject us.

At the end of the paper, I've inserted a Norman Fischer quote from his new book *Nature*: "Science lacks humanity when it misses a sense of play and rhyme—when it forgets that eye and world are one and there is no knowledge, only discussion; when it loses sight of humankind as Nature's extrusion, Nature's way of creating a paradox, linguistic pleasure, and novel modes of distraction and destruction which were engraved, as potential, in the first molecule of rugged and ragged life; when it fails to see itself in every rock and tree and star." Those are the final words of the paper.

The rest of it is far from the way I usually think about this bird music—I'm more used to playing in and around the mockingbird song as you and I do with it here in this piece.

SN: And it's very open. I like it.

DR: Harmonically, if you were to analyze what we're doing here, many of our pieces seem to just present an *Ooh Oh, Oh* and not resolve or go through a series of chords anywhere, which keeps you suspended in the moment.

SN: Suspended on our wings.

DR: It's a Wagnerian trick. That's how he invented movie music before movies. Wagner liked to have like all these churning chords suspending, holding you where the dragons are coming in, the clouds ...

SN: But we're doing it in a much more benign mode than Wagner.

## 8) DARK EYES DREAM: NOT PIANO, NOT RUSSIAN

SN: On to "Dark Ice Dream." After all the subterranean and jungle environments, this feels like a drink of cool water.

DR: It's always fun to play an instrument you don't usually play, and then to surprise yourself by ...

SN: ... sounding good on it!

DR: ... but also doing something you wonder why people don't do. The piano has these fixed notes. You can't bend them, but on the electronic piano, you can bend anything you want with pitch bend. And you never hear people bending piano sounds on a synth, only with a synth sound. And you're playing these very humpback whale-like slides on the violin.

I sent this piece to Jeff Goldberg, the great pianist I sometimes play with, and said, "I'm sorry, I'm playing your part here, don't get mad." And he goes, "No, it sounds great." Serious pianists hate fake pianos, but he was applauding the mix! It wasn't something I thought about doing before I suddenly did it. It was created in the moment, influenced perhaps by Messiaen. These kinds of arpeggios that we were taught were somehow dissonant, but if you've listened to enough of it, it just becomes normal. I'm happy we were allowed to put this in when playing something I'm not supposed to know how to play.

SN: This was the first piece we recorded on the first day.

DR: And the title—I was thinking about Andrei Voznesensky's poem, "Darkmotherscream," which is one word in Russian. I once heard him do this spontaneously on an old ship in the harbor in Oslo, Norway, at the Oslo International Poetry Festival in 1986. I was working there. He just got up and started reciting it as I think he often did throughout his life. And then you and I said something about ice. We played around with our titles—also a collaborative effort. This was a result of that.

## 9) SWAGTIME: DRESSING DOWN

SN: Yes. It felt wonderful. Shall we go to the next? "Swagtime" is your solo. It's a solo because we'd been working for some time and I had to go to the bathroom. And while I was gone for a couple of minutes, you were just noodling and doodling on your instrument, but it turned out to be a beautiful piece. Really nice.

DR: Thanks. Sometimes I feel I'm dressing up my music too much. All kinds of things happening, new sounds, nature sounds, effects, other things. Sometimes it's nice to play alone and just be there. I don't think I've ever recorded a bass clarinet solo piece alone like that.

SN: Well, it works.

DR: We should do more. It's not pushing the instrument with weird effects and weird techniques; it's simply playing it. And why did you give it this title again? "Swagtime."

SN: Larry Livingston thought of the name after hearing the piece. It's a combination of swing, swagger, swing time, swag time.

DR: Right. And swag is the extra gift you get, like the free clarinet solo.


## 10) UNDERTOW: SET OUR PURPOSES ASIDE

SN: Now we're up to "Undertow."

DR: That was a real duet between violin and what some would call a contrabass clarinet. It's also called a contralto clarinet because it's in the key of E flat, but it has this real powerful, thrumming kind of centering quality when you play it. For a year and a half, I've had it out here in the studio. I haven't put it away because it's such a pain to take apart. It's great to have this resonation in the room.

SN: It was so cool at this point in the album to have this pure duet of our two voices. No birds, no electronics; just us. It has a slow, bluesy quality, like an extended, flowing conversation. It's great to have this in the second-to-last spot on the album—if you think of the album as a journey.

DR: Yes, some people might listen to it from beginning to end the way we once imagined music should be listened to. It's nice to think about forming a more epic structure that way. At the same time, we know that music today is picked and chosen: put this song here, that one there, and all music is supposed to be filed and categorized by purpose.

SN: Well, we can just set utilitarian purposes aside and take them out with the garbage.

DR: My students always ask when they hear something: "What is this music for? What would you do with it?" Of course, that's not the right question to ask. Everything is not for something else. It's *The Art of Is.* It just is.

SN: Yes, exactly. We do it to do it. That's why, when Moses met God on the mountainside, Moses asked, "What should I call you?" And God said, "I am that I am."

DR: Exactly.

SN: I wrote about Moses years ago, sort of a Blakean prose poem version of that story. The task he took on was to go back to the city of drudgery, to free the slaves, to convince people that they can say, "I am that I am"—that's not just a name of one superbeing but what everybody can stand up together and say. I am that I am, and here we are together. Then combine that theme with the South African idea of *Ubuntu*. I have my being through your being, you have your being through my being, and we're in this together. That's the basis for something. That's a lot of fancy talk for what we're doing, but when we have this conversation in pure sound, it feels like we are plowing that field.

DR: Indeed.

SN: Back to listening to the album as a continuous whole. This was the way of listening to music in my long-ago youth, which I'm still perpetuating: the idea that you put on a record, lie on the floor, and listen to it from beginning to end. The album has a structure; it's one thing.

DR: Does no one do that anymore? Do people just not have the time? Or are they too distracted?

SN: I do it. And in this time of the COVID-19 pandemic, I've been listening to this album to edit and master it. I spent a lot of time taking walks with little earbuds on, listening to the flow between the pieces and thinking of it as a complete work. We talked earlier about the Beatles and their singing in just intonation. But these great albums, like *Sergeant Pepper's Lonely Hearts Club Band* or *Abbey Road*, were integral wholes. They weren't collections of songs; they were composed as albums meant to be listened to from beginning to end. And they work that way. Some of the process of editing this album was just shaving off or adding half a second of silence to the end of a piece. That way, the amount of silence from one piece to the next feels right as a transition. It's not piece, piece, piece, piece. It's a continuous flow with transitions.

DR: Yeah. I think the whole arrangement shows the effort you put into it to give it this quality. I wish I spent more time listening to music like that. I tend to pick and choose things. I get impatient, mostly listening to music when I'm driving somewhere in the car, and I don't drive anywhere at the moment. So I'm not doing it. I extract things, trying to figure out what someone's doing with a particular system. I don't spend the time I feel like I should to take it all in.

SN: When driving, I often have the iPhone shuffle on. I have 20,000 cuts of pieces of every genre of music imaginable. I never know what's coming next—all sorts of interesting transitions. I hear a few harsh transitions that don't feel good, but I get an amazing number of transitions where it almost feels compositional. Going from Bach to Sonny Rollins at this moment feels absolutely wonderful. Still, I love the traditional album. When you listen to the *Goldberg Variations*, it's thirty pieces one after another, with the transitions. I remember Glenn Gould talking about how he paced the truly great second recording of the *Goldberg Variations* just before he died. He was talking about tempos and transitions. Gould was meticulous, anal-compulsive, and had the chops to realize his ideals of the piece. He played with the tempos of each movement so that each was some multiple of the previous one and that they dovetailed together in interesting ways. He timed the pauses between movements.

DR: I feel like I'm listening to everything wrong, that I should spend more time with each sound. I feel wrapped up in the contemporary tendency to jump from here to there and mix this with that. This restlessness is of the moment.

SN: On the web now, even in a semi-reputable publication like *The New York Times*, they'll have two paragraphs of a story but then a "jump" to tempt you to click on some completely different story. Below the jump, they'll continue the story. If you want to read a story of twenty paragraphs, the attention economy wants you to constantly stop reading this *now* and *jump* to something else and jump to something else and jump to something else.

DR: A long-form story online is something that takes more than four minutes to read!

SN: It's insane. I think part of what one does in music, whether the music is fast or slow, is to get people to slow down. To slow down, to have patience, is to enhance consciousness. Here we are, two musicians in a conversation, so let's pursue the conversation without jumping to something else and then something else. It's worth paying attention to, trusting that life is long enough. Even though life is short, it's also long enough to have some conversations that go on for a while and are worth following.

DR: Yes. We all *do* have the time for this. You have to do it instead of jumping around. The time we spend on any one thing is no one's fault but our own. But at least this conversation we're having now is going on, and I think we have the final piece.

## 11) TEATRO PARADISO: *NAMU* TO *NOOSH*

SN: The final piece is coming, "Teatro Paradiso," where the dialogue gives way to growling and shouting!

DR: Hey, you finally got me to bring out my voice, to come in out of this deep and very rhythmic environment. Playing the contralto clarinet centers me.

SN: Interesting, hearing this. We talked about how the earlier piece was called "Malūma," but this was the piece where I actually was singing "Maluma."

DR: That's good. You don't want to give it all away and make it all make sense. This goes back to the famous Codona connection, and how much I was influenced by this group. At the beginning of side B of their first album, they're playing these unusual instruments, and in the middle of it, Naná Vasconcelos says "*Namu!*" They play another sound, and he says "Namu!" again. I asked Collin Walcott about it. He said, "Oh, that means 'more.'"

SN: In *The Art of Is*, I talk about the *naamunaamuna*. *Namu* in Arabic means "Yeah!" The griots in West Africa, the epic singer-improvisers of long-form genealogical poetry, would have an assistant or coworker who's called the *naamunaamuna*, whose job is to shout "*Namu!*" at regular intervals throughout the epic, usually at the ends of verses. There is a similar thing in African American churches with a tradition of call and response. The preacher is preaching and the people are shouting, "Yeah! Preach it, brother!" Or in rap, they'll have the hype man—it's the same kind of thing. With our Western idea of performers, we think here's the griot, who's *the* performer, *the* artist, *the* person with the chops, the technique, and so forth. But that technique is dependent on the *naamunaamuna* shouting out, marking the verses. These kinds of exclamations, the so-called gibberish of the voice, are so interesting. It's fun to end the album with these purely delightful vocalizations and breath sounds.

DR: You just sent me to look up the same thing in the Persian poetry of Hafez. Not content with writing one book about nightingales in Berlin, I wrote more after what happened the last time we were out there. It's all wrapped up in Hafez stories. By the end, I'm writing my own Hafez lyrics, which have to be translated back into Persian. This is coming out in a book and we had such a hard time getting the Persian to work. It ends with this poem:

> Under the nightingale's song
> Everyone is gone except you and I
> The night is cold but we are warm
> As warm as long as the nightingale sings—
> Forever.

And then my good friend Lima Vafadar who's translating this says, "You have to end with an invocation in Persian followed by *Noosh*! *Noosh* means exactly what you're talking about." She says, "Do you want to end with *Noosh*?" I say, "Yes. I want to end with *Noosh*."

SN: Yes!

DR: You see, the world has these sounds. Back when I first heard *Namu!* I guess I knew one day I'd be putting in these words because language, as you know, means the most when we don't even know what we're saying. Sounds are taking us out into the world, into the world of birds.

In "Teatro Paradiso," I put in a bird, a starling. I grabbed some starling recordings from xeno-canto. The starling is this common bird, often overlooked. People think it's just a loud noise but it's like totally weird, cool electronic music. I looked at what's in this particular starling sound and it says, in German, this is a recording of the starling imitating the black kite (which has a great name, the *Schwarzmilan*) and then a chicken. And so, you have the starlings imitating sounds in the middle of their songs, something that upset Noam Chomsky because he didn't think birds could do stuff like that. The birds are cutting and pasting and sampling and learning from each other. Just like we're trying to learn from them.

SN: Yes, as in that film we both saw recently, *Dancing with the Birds*, in which there's the bowerbird imitating machinery then imitating the sound of children playing in the nearby village.

DR: Crazy. Evolution produces a lot of play and experimentation.

SN: Yes! It felt wonderful to end the album in this spirit of play and childlike stuff, even though it was done in a low gravelly voice. You can often be playful in a low voice!

DR: Tom Waits, introducing the band: "These boys are all

from good families, but there's something about their ways that just ain't quite right." I've always wanted to say that.

SN: I loved what we did today, reacting to each piece. These may be some of the most detailed program notes for any album ever. It's the spiritual program notes—excavating thoughts that came up through these pieces.

DR: It was good to be talking about the music, a kind of music that's often presented with no information. It's actually very interesting.

SN: With this kind of music, whatever kind of music this is, you're often tempted to say there's no information because we didn't have a plan; we just stood there and played. But, in fact, without any effort at all, we unearthed in conversation a lot of information about this music and a huge number of influences on both of us. We packed a great deal in here.

DR: That we did. It's really fun.

*These conversations were recorded on Feb 18, Feb 25, and March 5, 2021.*

Special thanks to Larry Livingston (who named several of our pieces, and the album itself), Leslie Blackhall, Ellen Burr, Jaanika Peerna, Lima Vafadar, Tyran Grillo.

# From This World, Another

David Rothenberg and Stephen Nachmanovitch

| | | | |
|---|---|---|---|
| 1 | **Fly, Sing, Dream** | 6:57 | Birds, clarinet, viola, percussion |
| 2 | **Aukuras** | 5:40 | Viola d'amore, bass clarinet |
| 3 | **For David Darling** | 4:29 | Violectra, clarinet, electronics, birds |
| 4 | **Bambuta** | 2:36 | Overtone flute, violin, birds, keyboard |
| 5 | **Malūma** | 4:06 | Clarinet, voice, percussion, birds, electronics |
| 6 | **Gravity's Wave** | 8:39 | Electronics, clarinet, violin, birds |
| 7 | **Beautiful Eggs** | 3:22 | Clarinet, violectra, birds, electronics |
| 8 | **Dark Ice Dream** | 2:10 | Violin, keyboard |
| 9 | **Swagtime** | 2:30 | Bass clarinet |
| 10 | **Undertow** | 6:34 | Violin, contralto clarinet |
| 11 | **Teatro Paradiso** | 4:32 | Voice, electronics, contralto clarinet, birds |

Total time: 52 minutes

Stephen Nachmanovitch: Violin, viola d'amore, viola, violectra, voice, percussion, birds, electronics.

David Rothenberg: Bb clarinet, bass and contralto clarinet, overtone flute, keyboards, birds, electronics.

Remotely recorded during the COVID-19 pandemic between Charlottesville, Virginia (Stephen) and Cold Spring, New York (David) on January 15 and 29, 2021

Music available on Bandcamp.

Musician and philosopher **David Rothenberg** wrote *Sudden Music*, *Why Birds Sing*, *Bug Music*, *Survival of the Beautiful*, and many other books, published in at least eleven languages. Born in 1962, he has more than thirty recordings out, including *One Dark Night I Left My Silent House* which came out on ECM, and most recently *In the Wake of Memories* and *They Say Humans Exist*. He has performed or recorded with Pauline Oliveros, Peter Gabriel, Ray Phiri, Suzanne Vega, Scanner, Elliott Sharp, Iva Bittová, and the Karnataka College of Percussion. *Nightingales in Berlin* is his latest book and film. Rothenberg is Distinguished Professor at the New Jersey Institute of Technology.

**Stephen Nachmanovitch** is the author *The Art of Is* and *Free Play*. Born in 1950, he graduated in 1971 from Harvard and in 1975 from the University of California, where he earned a Ph.D. in the History of Consciousness for an exploration of William Blake. His mentor was the anthropologist and philosopher Gregory Bateson. In the 1970s he was a pioneer in free improvisation on violin, viola, and electric violin. He has presented master classes and workshops at many conservatories and universities, and has had numerous appearances on radio and television, and at music and theater festivals. He has collaborated with other artists in music, dance, theater, and film, and has developed software melding art, music, literature, and computer technology.

Made in the USA
Middletown, DE
09 September 2024

60039279R00066